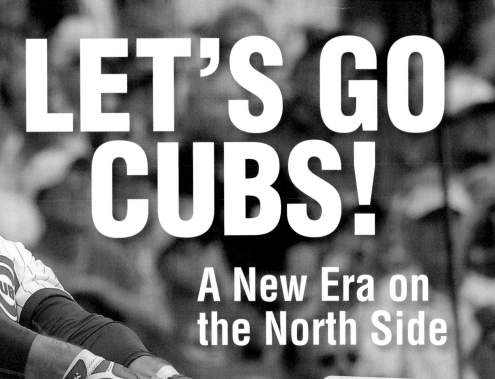

LET'S GO CUBS!

A New Era on the North Side

W9-BER-508

Daily Herald

dh **dailyherald.com**

(George LeClaire/Daily Herald)

This book is available in quantity at special discounts for your group or organization. For further information, contact:

Triumph Books LLC
814 North Franklin Street
Chicago, Illinois 60610
Phone: (312) 337-0747
www.triumphbooks.com

Printed in U.S.A.
ISBN: 978-1-62937-397-3

Daily Herald
Douglas K. Ray: Chairman, Publisher and CEO
Scott T. Stone: President/Chief Operating Officer
Colin M. O'Donnell: Senior Vice President/Director of Content
John Lampinen: Senior Vice President/Editor
Jim Baumann: Vice President/Managing Editor
Tom Quinlan: Assistant Managing Editor/Sports
Contributors: Bruce Miles, Mike Imrem, Barry Rozner, Travis Siebrass, Tim Broderick, Jeff Knox, Joe Lewnard, Mark Welsh, Daniel White, Steve Lundy, Brian Hill, Morgan Timms

Interior Design: Patricia Frey
Cover Design: Andy Hansen

Front cover photos by Mark Welsh/Daily Herald (Kris Bryant), Joe Lewnard/Daily Herald (Joe Maddon, Anthony Rizzo and Jake Arrieta), and John Starks/Daily Herald (Addison Russell)
Back cover photo by Mark Welsh/Daily Herald

CONTENTS

INTRODUCTION

By Bruce Miles

The 2015 Chicago Cubs provided their fans with one of the most fun and memorable rides in recent memory.

It was a ride engineered by manager Joe Maddon, a white-haired gentleman with big glasses who embodies the term "young at heart."

Speaking of young, the ride was made more memorable because of the innocence of youth. Several young players came up and contributed to a season that saw the Cubs win 97 games, up from their victory total of 73 the previous year. The Cubs eventually fell to the New York Mets in the National League championship series, but clearly a new era had dawned, an era of hope and optimism fueled by an infusion of young talent perhaps unprecedented in team history.

Entering 2016, expectations and excitement were ratcheted up through the roof. The Cubs had one target in mind: winning the World Series. They also found themselves the target of other teams who no longer would be surprised by this young bunch.

Enter Maddon with the perfect response: "Embrace the target." The saying, found everywhere around the Cubs from blackboards to t-shirts, is a clever phrase in which Maddon encourages his team to embrace the target of high expectations and to embrace being the target.

"To 'embrace the target,' what does that mean?" Maddon asked Day 1 of spring training. "You talk about the expectations, the word 'pressure' that is attached to it, which I believe are really positive words. So you take those concepts or those thoughts, and what does that lend to, what does that lead to? To me that leads to really focusing on the day, focusing on the process of the day, and the process needs to be our anchor.

"People are saying really nice things about us. That's good. But at the end of the day, we have to take care of our own business."

The Cubs took care of business in a big way to start this season. They ran out to a 25-6 start, the best by a Cubs team since the world-champion 1907 squad. The Cubs hit their high-water mark of 27 games over .500 (47-20) on June 19.

As all teams do, the Cubs slumped a bit at the end of June and the beginning of July, but one thing remained clear: This is a team chock full of young talent, and it should be a force for years to come.

Cubs right fielder Jason Heyward signs autographs for fans before a game. (Mark Welsh/Daily Herald)

One bit of evidence backing that argument was that the Cubs placed seven players on the National League all-star team, including 22-year-old Addison Russell, 24-year-old Kris Bryant and 27-year-old Anthony Rizzo.

To Maddon, having these players take part in the all-star game could lead to success breeding even more success.

"I think it means a lot," Maddon said. "First of all, individually, and I've talked about it before, what it does for your own personal self-esteem is very valuable. There's a lot of fan acceptance within that. There's some peer acceptance within that. You've wanted to play since you're a kid, you're an all-star, man. That's pretty sweet stuff. So I have to believe everybody that is involved and gets selected should feel some kind of a bump internally regarding confidence. They should, and I believe that they will."

As the season neared the 100-game mark, Rizzo and Bryant were strong contenders for the Most Valuable Player Award.

On top of that, the Cubs this year brought up outfielder Albert Almora Jr., 22, and pitcher Carl Edwards Jr., 24. Infielder Javier Baez, 23, has contributed with power at the plate and dazzling glove work in the field.

The Cubs have done it without the services of a couple other key young players because of injury. Catcher-outfielder Kyle Schwarber, 23, hit a monster blast on top of the right-field video board last year to help seal the Cubs' victory over the hated St. Louis Cardinals in the National League division series. Schwarber went down in April of this season with a season-ending knee injury.

Outfielder Jorge Soler, 24, an opening-day starter, has missed significant time this year with a hamstring injury.

Cubs manager Joe Maddon greets fans during the annual Cubs Convention at the Sheraton Grand Chicago.
(Daniel White/Daily Herald)

The future is bright for the young Cubs infield. From left, Addison Russell, Javier Baez, Anthony Rizzo and Kris Bryant. (Joe Lewnard/Daily Herald)

The Cubs had a few veteran all-stars as well. Jake Arrieta, the reigning Cy Young Award winner, made his first all-star team at age 30. Earlier this year, Arrieta authored his second career no-hitter, a gem at Cincinnati. He tossed a no-hitter at the Los Angeles Dodgers last August.

Left-hander Jon Lester, 32, made his fourth all-star team, and his first in the National League. Super utility man Ben Zobrist, the "old man" of the bunch at 35, made his third All-Star Game, his first in the NL, as a starter at second base. Zobrist was a key to the Cubs' hot start to this season. Center fielder Dexter Fowler, the sparkplug in the leadoff spot, was named to his first all-star team, but he could not play because of a hamstring injury.

Fowler again demonstrated his importance to the team when he homered, doubled, walked and singled in his first game off the disabled list.

So the question remains: Is this kind of early success sustainable? To Maddon it is.

"It's very sustainable," he said. "It's sustainable for years. Obviously, keeping guys well is important. These kids, I keep telling you, are going to be better. Put on your scout's cap and project what they look like in a few years. If you like them right now, that's great. They're going to get better."

In other words, buckle up. The ride is just beginning. ■

Kris Bryant and Anthony Rizzo combined to launch 46 home runs through the first half of the 2016 season. (Mark Welsh/Daily Herald)

BASH BROTHERS

Bryant/Rizzo Combo a Dream Match for Cubs

By Matt Spiegel | May 21, 2015

Watching Kris Bryant and Anthony Rizzo hit back to back in the late innings once recently, I longed for context. What do the Cubs have here?

As an opposing manager, I would hate the sight and thought of them. Consecutive excellent hitters (one from the right and one from the left) would get mental bullpen wheels turning rapidly.

Rizzo's remarkable progress against left-handed pitching has simplified things; it doesn't matter if you strategize with handedness against him. His excellence against lefties the last year and change has brought his career splits almost even.

But despite a decreased need to burn relievers, where do these two stand among the most daunting back-to-back LH-RH combos in the game?

We'll wait for a larger sample to base it on numbers alone. But I spoke to a pro scouting source from a current MLB team to get his opinions. He put Bryant and Rizzo up there with the very best.

As Joe Maddon stays consistent in batting his pitcher eighth (he's done it every game), batting

second and third is the new third and fourth. The best guys hit there, ideally with the ninth hitter and leadoff man on base more often than other teams.

Based on the average number of plate appearances by lineup position in a National League season, this should add 40 or 50 PA combined by the end of the year.

Bryant and Rizzo are hitting second and third nearly every game now. As of Thursday, Rizzo had started 10 games in the 2-hole, and 29 in the 3-spot. Bryant started 17 times at cleanup, but has hit second 11 times, and third 3 times.

Jorge Soler hit in one of those spots for 22 combined games, but has settled into fifth or sixth.

Cubs' batters are the worst in the eighth slot, by far. Other than pinch hitters (usually one of the catchers) it has all been pitchers. Their collective On Base + Slugging (OPS) of .289 is more than 200 points worse than any other team.

Meanwhile, their ninth-place hitters are leading others in almost every statistical category, though not by as wide a margin as the eighth hitters trail.

That production from the ninth position should grow if Addison Russell stays there and delivers on his promise.

At leadoff, Dexter Fowler has been good. Cubs No. 1 hitters are second to Miami (and amazing Dee Gordon), in OPS and most other categories.

So the table is being set for one of the most fearsome hitting combos of 2015.

The scout and I tried to keep current health and current production in mind, and we tried to be as specific as possible about where certain hitters are at this point in the season. Guys such as Troy Tulowitzki, Chris Davis and Robinson Cano would not get votes based on past performance.

He requested anonymity, and ranked the best RH/LH back-to-back hitters this way:

1. Matt Carpenter/Matt Holliday, Cardinals
2. Joey Votto/Todd Frazier, Reds
3. **Bryant/Rizzo, Cubs**
4. Howie Kendrick/Adrian Gonzales, Dodgers
5. Yunel Escobar/Bryce Harper, Nationals
6. Mike Moustakas/Lorenzo Cain, Royals
7. Prince Fielder/Adrian Beltre, Rangers
8. Nelson Cruz/Kyle Seager, Mariners
9. Alex Rodriguez/Mark Teixeira (S), Yankees
10. David Ortiz/Hanley Ramirez, Red Sox

Pretty good company. He almost went with Ryan Zimmerman over Escobar, and the truth is that Harper plus anyone is a good answer.

The Cubs now stand seventh in the NL in runs scored, sixth in OPS, second in walks, and second in stolen bases. Part of that high walk rate is because they take a lot of pitches.

Rizzo is pretty well established as one of the game's best lefty sluggers. It's possible the league will find a weakness in Bryant and word will get around, but odds are this continues to be the kind of pair a team dreams of having. ■

Kris Bryant and Anthony Rizzo are a force batting back-to-back in the Cubs' lineup, and should be for years to come. Bryant is 24 years old and Rizzo is 27, with both under team control for several years to come. (Joe Lewnard/Daily Herald)

A SIGN OF THINGS TO COME

This End Only Beginning for Cubs

By Barry Rozner, dailyherald.com | October 22, 2015

The morning after clinching a playoff berth, Theo Epstein talked of making the most of this opportunity despite the long odds the Cubs had already overcome.

Yes, it was great to arrive ahead of schedule, but once you're in it's important to take advantage because you never know when the next chance may occur.

And when you look at it objectively, the Cubs got all they could have out of this postseason.

The Cubs were swept out of the 2015 postseason by the better team and it ended unceremoniously at Wrigley Field with an 8-3 drubbing, a thorough beating from the Mets to finish the NLCS in the minimum number of required games.

The Mets scored first in every game, scored in the first inning of every game and outscored the Cubs 21-8 for the series — and it could have been worse.

As the Mets recorded the final out in the bottom of the ninth, the Cubs and their fans were forced to watch the Mets' celebration on a field that has seen so many celebrations this year, during what felt like the rebirth of a franchise.

Several players stayed a few minutes in the dugout, watching the winning team dance toward the World Series, wanting to pocket that wretched feeling for use somewhere down the road.

The fans, so loud for so many months, filed out slowly and quietly into another October night, still waiting for the year that ends in the biggest "W" of all.

It's a cruel finish for the Cubs after a remarkable season, but nevertheless a sweet tease for what the

Members of the Cubs acknowledge the fans after losing to the New York Mets in Game 4 of the 2015 National League championship series. (John Starks/Daily Herald)

future holds for a very young and talented group.

"I don't know how you can be disappointed in anything our players have done this year," said manager Joe Maddon. "Our players have done nothing but make me proud this year."

Those without any vision – who can't see past their own cynicism – will label this season a failure, forgetting they probably picked the Cubs to finish last in 2015.

The same old people will say the same old things about the Cubs not doing enough at the trade deadline, being too cheap to spend money and failing miserably at the management level.

They'll forget the Cubs won 97 games when they were supposed to be — essentially — a .500 club.

Of course, these are the same people who have trashed Epstein's plan at every turn, unable to see it coming together.

And now after embracing it for a few weeks, it will be the same story again.

They'll not acknowledge a huge step forward and that every moment the Cubs experienced in the postseason will help them in the future, up to and including their inability to compete in the NLCS.

How bright is the future?

The Cubs have six more years — at worst — of Anthony Rizzo, Kris Bryant, Kyle Schwarber, Addison Russell and Javier Baez.

Six more years — and that doesn't even include Jorge Soler, who will be here at least another five.

"I often look out on the field and I look at short, third, and left field," Maddon said. "I'll see KB, Addison, and Schwarber, and I think, 'Wow, to think about the level of experience that these guys have had to this point and where they've gotten us already, that's pretty impressive.'

"You look in right field, you might see Soler out there. You might see Baez at second base. I think we played five rookies in one game this year in Milwaukee. So that's not lost on me by any means.

"This is just the beginning. This is just the beginning for these guys. As our guys learn the game even better … that's going to be really exciting to watch over the next couple of years."

Most of those players just got here. Some of them are already very good. And they don't know a thing yet about how to compete at the big league level.

Imagine how good they'll be in two or three years.

"These guys have done a great job," said veteran starter Jon Lester. "They play well beyond their age and well beyond their years in this game, and that's only going to help us in this organization for years to come."

But they weren't good enough this year and it had nothing to do with curses or ghosts, fouls balls or goats. They simply didn't have the pitching to compete with New York, pitching Epstein had intended to pursue this off-season even before they fell short against the Mets.

They will have to think more in terms of manufacturing runs and better defense in October, balancing that with a desire to play long ball at a time when big bats are increasingly hard to find.

Unlike defeats of the past, however, this is merely the end of the beginning, rather than the beginning of the end.

The Cubs didn't take one shot with backloaded contracts and terrible deals. They didn't mortgage the future or waste their capital by giving up on young players to acquire someone who would help for a single October.

They built a team from scratch, arrived a year early and fell eight victories short of finishing it off.

Not bad for a start. ∎

Clockwise: Cubs manager Joe Maddon talks to his infield after taking starting pitcher Jason Hammel out of the game in the second inning against the New York Mets during Game 4 of the NLCS. (Steve Lundy/ Daily Herald); Maddon shows his appreciation of the crowd after the Cubs were swept in four games by the Mets in the NLCS. (John Starks/ Daily Herald); Cubs left fielder Kyle Schwarber misses a line drive off the bat of Mets shortstop Wilmer Flores in Game 4 of the NLCS. (Steve Lundy/Daily Herald)

KEY PIECES

Chicago Cubs Make Sense in How They're Spending Their Dollars

By Mike Imrem, dailyherald.com | December 8, 2015

Baseball money has become mind-boggling, and there's enough to go around.

All any of the 30 major-league teams needs to contend for a championship is to allocate their considerable assets wisely.

The Chicago Cubs appear to have done that by agreeing to a couple of so-called bargain contracts with a couple of so-called bargain free agents.

Veteran pitcher John Lackey: two years, $32 million. Versatile position player Ben Zobrist: four years, $56 million.

Yes, those are bargains in this affluent era of the game.

The Cubs also sent the $40 million left on Starlin Castro's contract — another bargain figure, right? — to the Yankees for lower-priced pitcher Adam Warren and a player to be named.

Major Leage Baseball is swimming in cash due to new-age revenue streams pumping into the game.

No team needs a $300 million payroll to win a World Series. The Dodgers have operated like that's what it takes and failed miserably.

The Royals won a World Series for considerably less. Anything above $100 million should be enough, and the Cubs will be well above that.

The Cubs' latest moves indicate that they have a winning mix: Money and brains.

Maybe luck, too.

Cubs president Theo Epstein and general manager Jed Hoyer caught a break when ace pitcher David Price turned them down to sign with the Red Sox.

Let's round off what the Cubs offered Price to $200 million, though it likely was a bit less.

Clockwise: Jason Heyward was a big off-season addition for the Cubs, signing an eight-year contract worth $184 million. (Joe Lewnard/Daily Herald); Ben Zobrist has been worth every dollar of his four-year, $56 million contract in 2016. (Mark Welsh/Daily Herald); John Lackey was signed as not only a veteran presence on the pitching staff but also as a blow to the St. Louis Cardinals, his former team and the Cubs' National League Central rival. (Mark Welsh/Daily Herald)

Price was more of a luxury than a necessity for the Cubs, considering that they already have Jake Arrieta and Jon Lester at the top of their rotation.

The Cubs needed a No. 3 as much as a No. 1 and that turned out to be Lackey, close to ancient but coming off an outstanding season with the Cardinals.

Lackey is one tough guy. He isn't afraid to hit a batter. He isn't afraid to take the ball every fifth day. He isn't afraid to go deep into a game.

Gritty pitcher to have on a team like the Cubs.

Then there's Zobrist, a player who can play every position on the field and maybe even pitch long relief if Cubs manager Joe Maddon asked that of him. They prospered together in Tampa Bay, Maddon and Zobrist did, and should be comfortable with each other in Wrigley Field.

Lackey and Zobrist fill needs at a combined commitment of $88 million, dozens of millions of dollars less than Price would have cost.

The Cubs then saved those 10s of millions — baseball would call them a pittance these days — in the Castro transaction.

It always made more sense to go after two pitchers, a No. 3 and No. 4, than to wind up with Price only.

Right now the Cubs' rotation lines up with Arrieta, Lester, Lackey and two from among Warren, Jason Hammel or Kyle Hendricks.

The Cubs still should have cash left over for a center fielder, bullpen help and more starting-pitching depth.

Maybe the Cubs would have had enough dollars for other reinforcements even after signing Price, but better that they didn't have to prove it.

Nothing is guaranteed now, of course. Lackey has to remain ageless. Others have to remain healthy. Everybody has to remain motivated.

Then the Cubs have to prove they're a team rather than just a big batch of talented individuals.

If they weren't before, the Cubs certainly are 2016 World Series contenders after Tuesday's flurry of activity.

All because they're turning dollars into sense. ■

The enthusiasm is mutual as the newly acquired Ben Zobrist greets fans at the Cubs Convention. (Daniel White/Daily Herald)

Anthony Rizzo and Jason Heyward are the primary left-handed bats in the Cubs' lineup, providing balance to the potent offense. (Mark Welsh/Daily Herald)

RIGHT ON TIME

Cubs Ready to Go from Good to Great

By Bruce Miles, dailyherald.com | December 16, 2015

Timing.

Think about the timing for both parties involved: Jason Heyward and the Chicago Cubs.

One year ago to the day in the same room of Spiaggia restaurant in Chicago, the Cubs were introducing their big free-agent prize, pitcher Jon Lester, as they expressed hope they could win in 2015.

This time, it was this year's free-agent prize, outfielder Jason Heyward, whom the Cubs are hoping can help take them to the next level after they advanced to the National League championship series in 2015.

"It's easy sometimes to sit back on the heels of a surprising 97-win season and be content with what you have and try to go out and do it again and contend again," said team president Theo Epstein, who also praised the business side of the Cubs' operation for making this winter's big financial commitments.

"But there was a real effort to go from good to great this winter and to capitalize on a moment in time when we have a lot of young, cost-controlled position players. We have Jon Lester and (ace pitcher) Jake Arrieta.

"(Business president) Crane Kenney and his people were great partners in trying to find creative ways to push some of the postseason money into this year's budget. We came up with some creative contract structures to allow us to add now because this is the right time strategically, with next year's free-agent market not being quite as deep as this year's."

The Cubs introduced the 26-year-old Heyward to Chicago after signing him to an eight-year contract worth $184 million. The timing works out pretty well for Heyward, too, as he can opt out after three years while still in his prime as a player.

Included is a $20 million signing bonus, which reports say is deferred, helping the Cubs financially until they get an expected huge TV deal at the end of this decade.

Epstein likened the Heyward signing to adding another "core" player to the one the Cubs already have with Anthony Rizzo, Kris Bryant, Addison

"It's easy sometimes to sit back on the heels of a surprising 97-win season and be content with what you have and try to go out and do it again and contend again." —Theo Epstein

Russell, Kyle Schwarber and Jorge Soler (who remains a Cub amid continuing trade speculation). The only member of the "core" the Cubs lost was Starlin Castro, whom they traded to the New York Yankees for pitcher Adam Warren.

Heyward took less money to come to the Cubs as opposed to staying with the St. Louis Cardinals – for whom he played only one year — or going to a team such as the Washington Nationals.

Being part of a young group was a main attraction, according to Heyward, a right fielder who is penciled in as the Cubs' center fielder unless or until Soler is moved.

"The St. Louis Cardinals are always going to be a great organization," said Heyward, who played for the Atlanta Braves from 2010-14. He was on the losing side of this year's National League division series against the Cubs.

"For me, and I keep hitting on this, being 26 years old, the fact that my contract will probably put me in any clubhouse longer than most people there, you've got to look at age. You've got to look at how fast a team is changing and how soon those changes may come about."

Heyward cited Cardinals veterans such as Yadier Molina and Matt Holliday "introducing" him to the St. Louis organization but that he could "look up in three years and see a completely different team," given the ages of those players and the contract status of others.

"Chicago really offers an opportunity to come in, be introduced to the culture." he said. "It's a young group of guys, but grow up with them and watch them grow up but still watch myself grow up and have some fun with some familiar faces for a long time."

Where Heyward bats in the Cubs' lineup will be a fun thing to watch, both during spring training and throughout the regular season. It's possible he could lead off, with recently signed second baseman Ben Zobrist batting second. Those two could flip-flop, or they both could find themselves hitting 5-6 on some days, as manager Joe Maddon likes to change things up often.

Last season the left-handed-hitting Heyward had a line of .293/.359/.439 with 13 home runs and 60 RBI for the Cardinals. For his career, he's at .268/.353/.431 with 97 homers and 352 RBI.

His career high in homers was 27 with the Braves in 2012, but Epstein cites former Red Sox right fielder Dwight Evans as a comparable player whose power could spike. At age 26, Evans hit 24 home runs and saw his power numbers increase to the tune of 32 homers at age 30, 32 at age 32 and 34 at age 35.

Heyward has batted up and down the lineup.

"I like where I'm hitting most when the team's doing the best, let's put it that way," he said. "If that means I'm hitting leadoff and the team's winning, I've done that. If the team's won, I'm all for it.

"I played for a 100-win team (with the Cardinals) and hit fourth down the stretch, and it worked out, as well. For me, where everybody's happy, I'm happy. And I understand what it takes to have to move around to accommodate maybe the next person or the next person."

On defense, Heyward is a three-time Gold Glove winner. Asked about his approach to defense, Heyward said simply: "I never take a play off." ∎

Jason Heyward's hitting has been a mixed bag early in his Cubs career, but his defense and baserunning are elite among his peers throughout the league. (Joe Lewnard/Daily Herald)

STARTING PITCHER

49

JAKE ARRIETA

Fresh Approach for Cubs Ace Arietta

By Bruce Miles, dailyherald.com | February 20, 2016

Can you really get too much of a good thing? When it comes to ace pitcher Jake Arrieta, the Chicago Cubs don't want to find out.

Arrieta enjoyed a season for the ages in 2015, when he went 22-6 with a 1.77 ERA and won the National League Cy Young Award.

In doing so, he logged a career-high 229 innings in the regular season, plus 19⅔ more in the postseason, including a complete-game shutout over the Pirates in the wild-card playoff game to propel the Cubs into the division series.

Arrieta's previous major-league high in innings pitched was 156⅔, set the previous year. He admitted to hitting the wall in the postseason, and for that reason the Cubs will take it a bit easier on him this spring and into the season.

No, Arrieta won't become a 5-inning pitcher, but if the team is leading big, he might come out after 6, or 7 tops.

"He understands why in spring training we're going to start him a little bit later, build into the season, be proactive regarding game situations, possibly not finishing a game with him this year

Jake Arrieta was traded to the Cubs after a disappointing start to his career for the Baltimore Orioles and has gone on to be on the of best pitchers in the game, winning the Cy Young in 2015. (Joe Lewnard/Daily Herald)

that we finished last year, with the lead, in an attempt to save and utilize him for the latter part of the season," manager Joe Maddon said.

"He gets it now. Guys like him who have never been through it before, you pretty much feel like you're invincible, you can do anything. We've all been through that.

"At least now he's had the experience of what it feels like to be in that position, and he knows it now firsthand. So my job should be somewhat easier in regards to harnessing him just a bit in regard to different moments during the season.

"I'm not talking about treating him like a kid. I'm not talking about backing off, just being a little more intelligent at the latter part of the game with the lead and when to get him out."

Arrieta seemed invincible last season, especially late. From Aug. 4 on, he went 11-0 with an 0.41 ERA, the lowest ERA for any pitcher from Aug. 1 on since the stat became official.

He dominated the Pirates in the wild-card game but admitted to being gassed, and he went 5⅔ innings in beating the Cardinals in Game 3 of the division series and 5 innings in losing to the Mets in Game 2 of the championship series.

Arrieta is a workout fanatic, combining Pilates and lifting as part of his conditioning. But he said Saturday he understands the need to back it down a bit.

"Last year I think my mindset was I want the game in the ninth inning every time out," he said.

"Looking back on it, toward the end of the season, my last 2 starts specifically, I had a noticeable point there where I could tell where I was a little out of gas.

"Going into this season, it's obviously very wise to monitor things early in the season to preserve things for October and so on and so forth. As nice as it is to complete games as a starter, it's even nicer to pitch meaningful innings in October, as I now know from last year's experiences."

Maddon said he and Arrieta have talked about the situation, and from Arrieta's perspective that kind of communication is one of the reasons he is accepting.

"Joe is the leader on this aspect," Arrieta said. "You got to check your ego at the door. It doesn't matter individually at this point because we were in the NLCS last year, and we expect to go one step further this year.

"If we're going to do that, there are certain sacrifices that have to be made, and I'm more than willing to make those sacrifices to be better for my team later in the season."

With the World Series possibly extending into November these days, Arrieta said the prize that awaits the winner then is more important than piling up stats and innings during the season.

"It looks good on paper, but a ring looks a little bit better at the end of November," he said. ∎

Jake Arrieta is known for his tenacity in all elements of the game — even on the bases — a rarity among starting pitchers.
(Joe Lewnard/Daily Herald)

Jake Arrieta is the ace of the Cubs' rotation and was selected for his first All-Star Game in 2016. (Joe Lewnard/Daily Herald)

THE RIGHT MIX

Why Cubs Believe in Creating Good Chemistry

By Bruce Miles, dailyherald.com | February 22, 2016

If baseball has a chicken-and-egg question, it's this: Does good team "chemistry" lead to winning, or does winning breed chemistry?

There's no doubt talent wins championships and that the Chicago Cubs' front office is one of the most analytical bunch of number-crunchers around.

But team president Theo Epstein and general manager Jed Hoyer value "character" players who add to good chemistry. That was evident recently in the clubhouse, where players such as Anthony Rizzo, Jason Heyward and Ben Zobrist were conducting lengthy sessions with media members and talking up the team concept.

"Theo does such a good job," said Rizzo, who has been in camp well before the reporting date for position players. "He brings in high-character guys. You see it already with Ben, Jay-Hey (Heyward) and (John) Lackey coming in. They just fit in. There are really no egos. That's what worked with us so well last year."

The Cubs won 97 games last season en route to an appearance in the National League championship series. By all accounts, that team enjoyed great chemistry as it won.

Joe Maddon is the manager and chief chemist — and sometimes alchemist — of the Cubs, and he believes good chemistry can be created.

"That's another good one," he said of the endless debate. "Me and Billy Bavasi (former major-league executive) used to go round and round about that. I always believed chemistry can be created because, after all, if you've never won before, where is the chemistry coming from? So I think the group that says that winning creates chemistry has never had to attempt to create it.

"What does that mean? We talked a lot about building relationships last year and creating trust, the interaction that leads to this open exchange of ideas. If you haven't had it before, how do you do it? You can't just say, 'I'm going to get a bunch of guys

The Cubs have great chemistry on and off the field, taking a cue from manager Joe Maddon to enjoy the journey. (Mark Welsh/Daily Herald)

in the room and they're going to win and then we're going to have chemistry.' I don't believe in that.

"I believe it can be intentionally created or done. So I'm a big proponent of the point that chemistry can be created. I know there's a lot of people who will disagree with that because they've never tried to do it before. Once that occurs, hopefully the winning attitude and culture follows."

Zobrist played for Maddon in Tampa Bay from 2006-14. He came close to a World Series title with the Rays before getting a ring last year with the Kansas City Royals, who obtained him during the season from the Oakland Athletics.

He weighed in on the two-sided coin of chemistry and winning.

"They go hand in hand," he said. "If you're playing well, you have good chemistry. And if you have good chemistry, you're more likely to play well. But I certainly think if teams win early on in a season, they feel like the chemistry is amazing regardless of whether you have a bunch of great guys in the clubhouse or not. You just get along better because you're winning.

"That being said, I do think there's a special group of personalities here that they all seem like they enjoy each other. They're very easy to get along with. And those kinds of players tend to want to win for each other. When you get out there and want to play for each other, you're more likely to sacrifice yourself in the moment you need to for the team. That's going to help the team win in the end. I think this team has it."

So please don't tell Anthony Rizzo chemistry is overrated. He will tell you differently.

"I don't think it's overrated at all," he said. "A lot of these (front-office) guys get paid to crunch numbers up top. They know how important it is to have chemistry.

"Every good team has that team chemistry. There are a few teams that win by talent, but the majority of teams, you look at the Royals last year, those guys played for almost 10 years coming up together. They're really good friends, and that's what we plan on doing." ∎

The youthful energy of the Cubs' roster is apparent, from pre-game drills, to in-game chatter and celebrations, to post-game parties in the clubhouse. (Mark Welsh/Daily Herald)

SURPRISE

Dexter Fowler Returns to Chicago Cubs

By Bruce Miles, dailyherald.com | February 25, 2016

Center fielder Dexter Fowler was one of the most popular players in the Chicago Cubs' clubhouse last year.

So it was no surprise Thursday that Cubs players applauded on the practice field in Mesa, Arizona, when Fowler joined them to say he was back.

The big surprise was that Fowler re-signed in the first place. He looked to be all but signed, sealed and delivered to the Baltimore Orioles as a free agent earlier this week.

But instead of signing for three years with the O's, Fowler took a one-year deal — plus a mutual-option season — to return to a team he helped get to the National League championship series last year.

Fowler gets $8 million this year, with the mutual option worth $9 million. There is a $5 million buyout if the Cubs don't exercise their option.

"Surprise," exclaimed Cubs president Theo Epstein to reporters as he announced the stunning deal on what turned out to be a big day for wheeling and dealing in Mesa.

As the primary leadoff hitter last year, Fowler put up a hitting line of .250/.346/.411 with a career high 17 home runs. He drove in 46. His 84 walks and 154 strikeouts also were career highs. In postseason play, Fowler went 10-for-36 (.278) with a pair of homers.

According to reports, Fowler surprised his teammates by showing up while manager Joe Maddon was addressing them.

"I owed it to the boys to tell them first," Fowler told the media. "My heart's here. I feel like the Cubs, they treated me with the utmost respect. With the off-season moves they made, you've got to go with what's comfortable."

Those moves were the signings of free agents Jason Heyward, John Lackey and Ben Zobrist.

Fowler added that news that he was signing in Baltimore was premature.

As Epstein put it: "He decided to go for the fit over the money. We're extremely appreciative of that. It means a lot. I think it says a lot about his teammates. It says a lot about Dexter, the manager, the coaching staff here, ownership."

The Fowler re-signing has the potential of changing a lot of things for the Cubs.

As they opened spring training, the plan was for Heyward to play center field. Heyward, who signed an eight-year, $184 million deal with the Cubs this winter, is a Gold Glove right fielder who spent most of his career in Atlanta before playing for the St. Louis Cardinals last season.

Although Epstein told reporters Heyward could still see time in center, it appears now the Cubs can put Fowler in center and move Heyward to his natural spot in right.

Youngster Jorge Soler was their primary right fielder last year, and the Fowler move could signal a trade of the right-handed-hitting Soler, or it could mean he will share left field with left-handed-swinging slugger Kyle Schwarber.

The Cubs originally got Fowler from Houston in a Jan. 19, 2015, trade for pitcher Dan Straily and infielder Luis Valbuena. Fowler was one of several notable free agents who were unsigned as spring training opened.

"Yeah, it's sickening," Cubs first baseman Anthony Rizzo said earlier this week. "I do stay in touch with him a lot. I love Dex. It'll work out for him …"

It looks like it worked out for everybody. ■

Leadoff man and center fielder Dexter Fowler shocked everyone by spurning the Baltimore Orioles and coming back to the Cubs for the 2016 season. (Steve Lundy/Daily Herald)

FIRST BASEMAN

44

ANTHONY RIZZO

Rizzo Among Best First Baseman in Baseball

By Bruce Miles, dailyherald.com | March 1, 2016

The National League has three bona fide superstars playing first base.

The Cubs' Anthony Rizzo is one of them. While Rizzo ranks behind the Reds' Joey Votto and the Diamondbacks' Paul Goldschmidt in wins above replacement (WAR) — 7.4 for Votto and Goldschmidt and Votto last year to 5.5 for Rizzo — he also has emerged in so many ways as the face of the Chicago Cubs franchise.

That's true of his on-the-field performance and his off-the-field charitable works.

Rizzo played in 160 games last season, putting up a line of .278/.387/.512 for an .899 OPS. He hit 31 homers, drove in 101 and was hit by 30 pitches. The 6-foot-3, 240-pound Rizzo also stole 17 bases.

He made the National League all-star team for the second straight year and was fourth in

Anthony Rizzo has been a premier first baseman in his five seasons with the Cubs, earning three all-star selections and growing into one of the most feared sluggers in the game. (Mark Welsh/Daily Herald)

voting for the Most Valuable Player Award, behind winner Bryce Harper, Goldschmidt and Votto.

Rizzo spent the early days of spring training picking the brain of outfielder Jason Heyward, the team's big free-agent prize. Now at the ripe old age of 26, Rizzo might find teammates coming to him for advice.

"I just look at is as conversation," he said. "The more information you can gather and process, the better off you are."

Rizzo may have stirred some waves at the end of the 2014 season when he said the Cubs' goal for 2015 season was to compete for the NL Central title. That was just as the Cubs were finishing '14 with a mark of 73-89.

Although they finished third in the Central last year, the Cubs had 97 victories, third most in major-league baseball.

Rizzo seems to have bought into manager Joe Maddon's approach about focusing on the "process" rather than the end result. So the talk isn't so bold this spring.

"I really feel like we're in the same position we were in last year," Rizzo said. "We know what we're capable of doing. It's about going in this year and doing exactly what we need to do again. My biggest thing is April. It's not easy playing at Wrigley in Chicago in April."

With Rizzo being a stalwart as far as playing time goes, there hasn't been much need for a "backup" first baseman on the Cubs. ■

Top: Anthony Rizzo has cemented his reputation as a great first baseman not only with his big bat but also with his trusty glove. He is one of the top defenders at the position in the league. (Mark Welsh/Daily Herald) Opposite: In 2016 Rizzo is on pace to top 30 home runs for the third consecutive season. (Joe Lewnard/Daily Herald)

SHORTSTOP

27

ADDISON RUSSELL

Russell Looks Like Mainstay for Cubs at Shortstop

By Bruce Miles, dailyherald.com | March 7, 2016

For a guy who played much of last year out of position, the Chicago Cubs' Addison Russell looked good.

Now settled in his natural place at shortstop, there are those who think the ceiling is unlimited for this 22-year-old.

Russell came up last April and played second because Starlin Castro was the mainstay at short. But after Castro slumped at midseason and was benched, Russell moved over and wasn't moved out until a hamstring injury in the division series forced him out for the championship series.

Despite the injury, Russell reflects fondly on 2015.

"I felt pretty confident in my abilities of being able to switch to a different position," he said during the early days of camp in Mesa, Arizona. "That's what Joe (manager Maddon) felt, too. I got the call-up and produced, then went over to shortstop and did the same thing.

Addison Russell is a terrific shortstop defensively, using his great range and athleticism to make both routine and amazing plays with consistency. (Joe Lewnard/Daily Herald)

"So a pretty good year all around."

Maddon believes Russell can win a Gold Glove at shortstop as early as this season. The advanced-metrics people love everything about Russell's defense: his fielding ability, arm strength and range.

At the plate, Russell has showed promise, but he's a work in progress. Last year he put up a batting line of .242/.307/.389 with 13 homers and 54 RBI. The Cubs would love to see Russell improve his on-base percentage and walk rate of 8 percent.

He struck out 149 times in 523 appearances for a strikeout rate of 28.5 percent, making him like other young hitters on the club.

But the biggest concern for Russell in the off-season was making sure his legs were good after injuring his left hamstring running out a triple in Game 3 of the NLDS.

"I pushed myself this year," he said. "I'm going to ask Bussie (strength coach Tim Buss) if he can push me a little bit this year as well so I keep that competitive edge and make sure my body's in shape.

"Strengthening itself, we're definitely working on more leg muscles and back muscles as well. Conditioning is going to take care of itself.

"You're grinding with these guys every single day and then you're presented with the opportunity of hopefully being able to go to the World Series and it being cut short by just an injury.

"This year I've definitely taken more precautions in making sure my body's ready for a long season."

Like Castro before him, Russell is now a young veteran.

"I've got almost a full year under my belt," he said. "They're all great guys in this clubhouse, so it's easier stepping into the season."

Unlike Castro, who was traded to the Yankees, Russell came up in a winning environment. This off-season, they added Jason Heyward, John Lackey and Ben Zobrist, all of whom have played on winning teams in the past.

"It's a pretty cool thing," Russell said. "With KB (Kris Bryant) and (Kyle) Schwarber coming in, and myself and putting more pieces into it and young talent as well, with Zobrist, and Heyward only 26 years old, and Lackey. Those are three key guys."

It will be interesting to watch where Russell regularly hits in the batting order. Last year he started in the ninth spot of the order 116 times.

Maddon likes to hit the pitcher eighth and create more opportunities for the ninth hitter to set the table for the big guys. If it goes that way again, Russell is OK with it.

"Joe already basically knows how it's going to go down," he said. "We're just like puzzle pieces. He puts us in. The 9-hole was an adjustment last year.

"I was looking at footage. I'm trying to get better in the 9-hole this year. I'll be excited to be in the 9-hole. I'll be excited to be in the lineup like anyone would be. But the 9-hole is nice for me. If I move up in the lineup, we'll make those adjustments." ∎

Addison Russell's bat has started to come around to complement his already stellar defense, with his power numbers up and patience at the plate greatly improved in 2016. (John Starks/Daily Herald)

RIGHT FIELDER

22

JASON HEYWARD

Heyward Brings Defense, Smarts to Right Field

By Bruce Miles, dailyherald.com | March 10, 2016

Not since the days of Andre Dawson can Cubs fans get as excited about the guy patrolling right field at Wrigley Field.

It looked like it wasn't going to be that way for a time this winter.

When Jason Heyward signed his eight-year, $184 million free-agent contract with the Cubs in December, he looked to be ticketed for center field, not his customary right.

But the surprise spring-training re-signing of Dexter Fowler to play center enabled the Cubs to move Heyward back to right.

That's a good thing.

Heyward is a three-time Gold Glove winner — in 2012 and 2014 with Atlanta and last year for the St. Louis Cardinals.

He seemed more than prepared at the beginning of spring training to embrace the challenge of

One of the most coveted free agents of 2015, Jason Heyward chose to sign with the Cubs over several competing teams.
(Mark Welsh/Daily Herald)

center field even though he's at home in right.

"Right field is pretty much me," he said. "I'm good there."

Heyward made a grand total of 3 errors in right last year after making just 1 the previous season in Atlanta. He possesses a strong arm and range in right.

But the Cubs didn't sign Heyward just to play defense. They got him to provide leadership and produce with the bat.

He had a batting line of .293/.359/.439 in 154 games last year with 13 homers and 60 RBI. His on-base percentage of .359 was his best since a .393 mark during his rookie season in 2010 with the Braves. The Cubs would love more power; Heyward's career high in homers (27) came in 2012, but they figure to get plenty of that from the likes of Anthony Rizzo, Kris Bryant and Kyle Schwarber.

Heyward experienced a big jump in his groundball rate from 2014 to 2015, as it went from 45.5 percent to 57.2. His flyball percentage dropped from 35.6 percent to 23.5.

The Cubs haven't been too hung up on stats when it comes to Heyward. They like what he brings in baseball smarts. He's been a good fit in the clubhouse, as he was last year in his only year with the Cardinals, who pride themselves on playing the game "right."

"That's what was cool about being in St. Louis," he said. "I fit right in with that, with that mold: just being myself, thinking the game, always trying to be a few steps ahead. Derek Jeter was always one of my favorite players growing up, and he always had that sixth sense on the field, and it's just something I took a liking to right away and saw how it helped him." ■

Top: Jason Heyward's defensive prowess and intelligent perspective stand out in the minds of Cubs' management. (Joe Lewnard/Daily Herald) Opposite: Despite struggles at the plate early in the 2016 season, Heyward brings the promise of a solid bat and great on-base numbers. (Mark Welsh/Daily Herald)

STARTING PITCHER

41

JOHN LACKEY

Lackey a Shrewd Pickup for Cubs

By Bruce Miles, dailyherald.com | March 19, 2016

Most of the talk about the Cubs' off-season centered on the signing of right fielder Jason Heyward to an eight-year, $184 million contract, and rightly so.

But one of the shrewdest moves engineered by Cubs president Theo Epstein and general manager Jed Hoyer might have been picking off free-agent pitcher John Lackey from their Gateway Arch rivals, the St. Louis Cardinals.

The 37-year-old Lackey came to the Cubs on a two-year, $32 million deal in December.

It's no secret the Cubs suffered a drop-off in quality in their rotation last year after Nos. 1 and 2 pitchers Jake Arrieta and Jon Lester. Lackey will slide nicely into the No. 3 spot this year.

Not only does Lackey give the Cubs some much-needed starting depth, but he also has world-championship experience, with the Angels in 2002 and the Red Sox in 2013.

The native of Austin, Texas, also is known as a tough, all-business competitor on the mound.

"Four out of five days I'm pretty laid-back and

In John Lackey, the Cubs found the rotation depth they needed. (Mark Welsh/Daily Herald)

having a good time," Lackey said as spring training opened in Mesa, Arizona. "When it's my day, we only get 30-some times to help the team. I take it pretty dang serious. I'm going to go get after it.

"I think (the approach) has helped me, for sure. It's not going anywhere. It's just there. It's kind of what it is."

Something has worked for Lackey in his big-league career, which began in 2002 with the Angels. His lifetime record is 165-127 with a 3.92 ERA.

He earned the win in Game 7 of the '02 World Series against the Giants, becoming the first rookie to do so since Babe Adams of the 1909 Pittsburgh Pirates.

For the Cardinals last year, he was 13-10 with a 2.77 ERA. His WHIP was a solid 1.21. He beat his friend and teammate Lester in Game 1 of the National League division series in St. Louis.

Cubs manager Joe Maddon has known Lackey for a long time, from their days together with the Angels.

"He's getting better," Maddon told reporters recently. "It starts with his delivery, and the next component is that he knows what he's doing out there. He'll never give in to a hitter. That has not changed."

Lester and Lackey are good friends on and off the field. Along with Cy Young winner Arrieta, all three are seen as leaders for a Cubs team that still features a lot of young players.

"The ways you win championships haven't changed," Lackey said. "We (he and Lester) both won a couple. Ultimately, we can bring some of those things here and if we can put it all together with some of this young great talent we have on this team, and get it done." ∎

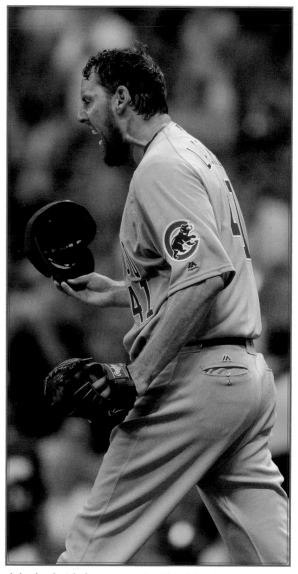

John Lackey is known as a tough, all-business competitor on the mound. (Mark Welsh/Daily Herald)

John Lackey brings valuable postseason experience to a Cubs team looking toward October. (Mark Welsh/Daily Herald)

MANAGER

'70
JOE MADDON

Maddon Focused on Journey of Season

By Bruce Miles, dailyherald.com | March 26, 2016

No, Joe Maddon's saying for this Cubs season isn't "remember the mime."

Never mind that few could forget Maddon bringing the sounds of silence into spring-training camp recently to liven up the daily stretch. He outdid even that a few days later with bear cubs.

But with Maddon, there are always words of wisdom and inspiration. This year, it's "embrace the target."

There's a nice double meaning there. Of course, the target for the Cubs is to get beyond where they went last year and into the World Series. Coming off a 97-win season and an appearance in the National League championship series, the Cubs also will have targets on their backs.

How to handle it all? Enter Maddon.

"There is a target," said the 62-year-old Maddon, entering his second year as Cubs manager. "It's much bigger than it was last year. I want it to continue to grow. When you say that, you also have to define it for your group. Really for me, in order to embrace the target properly and understand that, you have to accept the fact that you have to really

Named the 2015 National League Manager of the Year, Joe Maddon hopes to take a new generation of Cubs to new heights.
(Joe Lewnard/Daily Herald)

> "We have not won a World Series in a century, so there is nothing to get complacent or cocky about. Bring that all on the table. Talk about it. Say it up front and work it from there. That's why I believe it's important to embrace the target." —Joe Maddon

beat to death 'process.' If you, on a daily basis, really attack the word 'process' and what it means, then you can more easily handle the expectations and pressure, all the items that build the target."

"Process" is another of Maddon's favorite terms. Although the Cubs have an end goal in mind, Maddon believes the end result takes care of itself by focusing on the day-to-day things and not getting caught up in outcomes.

"Our relentless execution of managing expectations, that equals our process," he said. "Without getting too academic, I try to put it into words our guys can understand. You run toward the fire as opposed to away from it. I want our guys to understand that. That's the way it is. It's great. It means you're good. We are good. Then how do we deal with this daily? I think you need to talk about it upfront.

"We have not won a World Series in a century, so there is nothing to get complacent or cocky about. Bring that all on the table. Talk about it. Say it up front and work it from there. That's why I believe it's important to embrace the target."

Maddon has spent the last month and a half drilling that into his players. It might be easier for them to embrace process than it is for Cubs fans, whose team has not won a World Series since 1908 or played in one since 1945.

In the early days of camp, Maddon acknowledged that he and his players are in an outcome-based business. At the end of the day, it matters if they've won or lost. At the end of the year, it matters whether they've reached and won the World Series.

"My point is that you take care of the seconds, the minutes and the hours, and the days will take care of themselves," he said. "Why would you want to focus on the end of the book as opposed to each sentence and each line? That's what I'm talking about regarding the process of this thing. The game ebbs and flows so much. The season ebbs and flows so much. Why would you be constantly focused on your record at the end of the year?

"But how do you arrive at a good outcome, a positive outcome? How do you define that? I'm into defining everything. My definition would be to do what I'm talking about so you achieve the outcome you're looking for."

So what does this look like on a baseball field day after day from April to October?

"He lets us relax and have fun," center fielder Dexter Fowler said during last year's playoffs. "That's huge. He doesn't get too uptight. He lets the veterans in the clubhouse manage the clubhouse, and he goes out and manages on the field. That's been working, and he's our manager for a reason. He's had success for a reason."

In his first year as Cubs manager and his first in the National League, Maddon gave us a good look at how his teams play ball and how he manages games and people. Some of those looks show up in the numbers. Others do not.

To wit:

- The Cubs ranked 14th of 15 NL teams last year in sacrifice bunts, with 32. Part of that stemmed from the pitchers having trouble laying down bunts. Part of it was that Maddon does not like to give away outs via the bunt.
- Cubs baserunners were sixth in the NL in stolen bases, with 95, showing that Maddon likes to put things in motion.

- Maddon is not afraid to ruffle feathers, but in doing so he tries to avoid "losing" a player mentally. He benched since-traded shortstop Starlin Castro during the season but reinstated him at second base. Castro, to his credit and perhaps because of the way Maddon handled him, responded by being one of the Cubs' most productive players down the stretch and rebuilding his value enough so that the Cubs could trade him. Maddon also took away pitcher Travis Wood's starting job, sending him to the bullpen, where Wood became an effective reliever.
- Rare was the day in August and September that the Cubs took a full on-the-field batting practice, an exercise Maddon calls overrated. That may have kept the players fresh, as the Cubs went 19-9 in August and 23-9 in September-October for a .700 winning percentage.
- Maddon led both leagues in successful replay reviews.
- Showing that he'd stand up for his players, Maddon was ejected five times last season. He also wasn't afraid to verbally rip up the "book" the Cardinals allegedly wrote on how to play baseball, as he launched into a shrewdly crafted postgame speech in September about how the Cubs would not back down.

Joe Maddon believes that a focus on process and day-to-day excellence will help the Cubs handle high expectations. (John Starks/Daily Herald)

This season is upon us, and of course Maddon already has thought of how the team should handle the "pressure" and "expectations" that come with it being on the cover of *Sports Illustrated* and widely picked to win the NL Central.

"What I'm really trying to have our players understand, our fan base understand and maybe all of humanity understand is that sometimes, most of the time, 'expectations' and 'pressure' are positive words," he said. "When there are expectations placed on you, that means there is probably something good, a carrot, at the end. When the word 'pressure' is utilized, same thing. It means you're in the situation where you have this opportunity to do something very special.

"Too many times, when you hear those two words, automatically, I think, people cringe about the negative component attached. Then all of sudden, you're supposed to cower and run away from them. I totally disagree with that. How do you battle expectations and pressure? You do that by the relentless execution of the process. You really have to make the process your primary objective.

"It's easier to approach the day that way. Outcome is really the enemy. The people who want to focus and dwell on outcomes all the time, that's where you feel pressure. That's where you feel expectations. To me, that's not really a good way to live in general." ■

JOE COOL

Festival of Maddon Working for Cubs

By Barry Rozner, dailyherald.com | March 26, 2016

The genius of Ozzie Guillen was his very nature, which was by definition a distraction.

At least when the White Sox were competing for something, Guillen kept the media thinking mostly about him and chasing whatever nonsense he was firing at the wall that day.

Of course, when it all went bad and the Sox were dropping like a rock, Guillen's troubles forced players to answer for the manager. That's the downside of the circus.

But it bears remembering that when they were good, Guillen had the focus on the manager's antics, relieving the pressure from the players, forcing all eyes on Guillen at all times.

It was effective and crucial, and though Guillen would never admit there was a method to the everlasting madness, he was at his best when the players could go about their day unburdened by the weight of expectations and attention.

Joe Maddon is slightly more transparent.

He requires his players embrace expectations, to understand the goal is to get better every day, every month, every season, which in this case means improving on a 97-win season.

The players should understand this, Maddon believes, but not dwell on it.

Thus, the circus known as the Chicago Cubs.

Nearly every day has brought something to keep the players' minds off the drudgery of spring training, and soon the drudgery of an interminable championship season. Whether it's clowns or bears or aging rock stars, the absurdity of it is entirely the point. Of course it's absurd. It's supposed to be.

The players laugh, the fans applaud and the media has no choice but to focus the cameras on the distraction of the day. With the national media watching every step the Cubs take, they concentrate on animals and jugglers, thinking more about the entertainment and less about Jake Arrieta's blister.

Both surprising and entertaining, Joe Maddon's methods and philosophy help set the Cubs apart. (Mark Welsh/Daily Herald)

Joe Maddon's unconventional methods saw jugglers, mimes and bears making appearances at the Cubs' 2016 spring training camp. (Daniel White/Daily Herald)

It's cute, if you like cute. Not everyone does.

"If everybody's (not) entertained, so be it," Maddon told reporters in Arizona. "That's just our way to start the day. We did that last year without nearly as much attention.

"It's just the way our venue sets up and the fact that we permit so much access. Everybody's able to see it."

Opposition teams are mumbling under their breath in other camps, already tired of the cuddly Cubs, everyone's choice to win the World Series, end the drought and include a manager's menagerie in the parade.

That's fine with Maddon, too.

"If people misinterpret it, honestly, that's their fault," Maddon said. "It's really just about the esprit de corps of the day. It has nothing to do with your work, except that I think your work can be better because you get off to a good start."

Let the rest of the National League worry about what the Cubs are doing, while they go about the business of slowly getting ready for the marathon that begins in a week.

But this is no slam dunk.

The Cardinals and Pirates will be right there again in the Central Division. The Mets have dominant pitching. The Nationals are quietly trying to get back in the conversation. The Diamondbacks had a huge off-season. The Dodgers believe they'll be in it again. And the Giants in an even-numbered year are looking for their fourth title in seven seasons.

San Francisco still remembers the way the Cubs took them apart in August last year and some of this may have been in a play a few days ago when the hot-running Madison Bumgarner had words with Jason Heyward.

Yeah, in a spring training game. Seriously.

Bumgarner reacted after Heyward apparently said something to Dexter Fowler standing on second base. Heyward said he was asking his teammate if the umpire got the call right. Bumgarner first thought the batter was talking to him, and then accused the Cubs of flashing signals from the bases.

In spring training?

If they were working on tipping pitches from second base, it's a good time to practice. And, by the way, it's not against the law. Whatever. It's an exhibition game.

"It was a misunderstanding," Heyward said. "No tipping of signs. I understand people would say, 'They wouldn't tell us anyway.' But believe it or not, that wasn't going on, especially not in a spring-training game.

"I wouldn't show up my teammate if they ever gave me the wrong sign."

For the love of Rick Wrona and all that's holy, this is spring training we're talking about here, but it gives you an idea of the intensity surrounding the Cubs and just one more reason the team has embraced the Festival of Maddon.

So while the hype swirls everywhere around the Cubs, they go about their business and seem to chuckle more than worry.

There are worse ways to start a long season. ■

Joe Maddon is as popular with Cubs fans as he is with the players he manages. (Daniel White/Daily Herald)

PRESIDENT OF BASEBALL OPERATIONS

THEO EPSTEIN

Epstein Makes Cubs Plan Come Together Right on Cue

By Barry Rozner, dailyherald.com | April 4, 2016

For the love of Todd Haney and all that's holy, the plan has taken shape nicely, regardless of how baffling it remains to a few.

The Chicago Cubs' plot to gut the team, rebuild the farm system and put in place a club that can make a run at the World Series every year for the next five or six seasons is troubling for those who can't fathom how this occurred right before their eyes -- even while seven remains more than six.

And the Cubs should know that those troubled souls will be on the offensive this season.

With every defeat, Theo Epstein will be a failure. With every injury, the Cubs will be a disaster.

And with every stumble, the Cubs will be the most overrated baseball team in the history of the game.

Get used to it.

There's a lot of unhappy folks right now because the plan has worked precisely how Epstein hoped it would.

He said it would take five years to rebuild the organization and field a competitive team, though it took only four to reach the NLCS.

The next step is winning the pennant and four more games beyond.

It could happen this year, but there's no guarantee. There never was. But just as Epstein imagined in Boston, the idea was to build something that would last and give the Cubs multiple shots at the big prize.

He didn't trade off valuable pieces for one shot at it. He didn't waste money for a single turn. He didn't make the mistakes Cubs executives had made for the last 30 years.

So some experts were mad when the Cubs didn't make a play for Albert Pujols or Prince Fielder.

They were mad when the Cubs tanked and drafted Kris Bryant and Kyle Schwarber.

They were mad when the Cubs took a flyer on Scott Feldman, and then mad when they flipped Feldman for Jake Arrieta and Pedro Strop.

After having been instrumental in ending the Boston Red Sox's World Series drought, Theo Epstein turned his sights to the Chicago Cubs. (George Leclaire/Daily Herald)

The Cubs' steady rebuilding efforts under Theo Epstein have gone precisely according to schedule. (Mark Welsh/Daily Herald)

They were mad when the Cubs traded Ryan Dempster for Kyle Hendricks.

They were mad when the Cubs traded Matt Garza for Justin Grimm, Neil Ramirez and Carl Edwards.

They were mad when the Cubs traded Andrew Cashner for Anthony Rizzo.

They were mad when the Cubs traded Jeff Samardzija and Jason Hammel for Addison Russell and Billy McKinney, insisting the Cubs didn't get enough.

They were mad when they didn't keep the likes of Aramis Ramirez and Alfonso Soriano.

And they were wrong.

So now they're uncomfortable, and if the Cubs don't win the World Series this year it will be called a colossal disaster, the likes of which, well, no one has ever seen before around these parts.

It's nonsense, of course. The plan wasn't about a single chance to win it all.

Maybe most amazing is that the Cubs have built this team without moving a single top-notch prospect, hanging on to Bryant, Schwarber, Russell, Jorge Soler and Javy Baez, even when so many called for trade-deadline deals that would have netted a two-month rental.

They still have McKinney, Albert Almora, Ian Happ, Gleyber Torres and Jeimer Candelario as chips to play when they go shopping for pitching help in June or July.

And it's been done with a transparency rarely seen in Chicago sports that should have made it easy to understand, explaining from the first news conference how they would go about doing it, that it would be painful, but that it would pay off in the end.

Nothing about it has been easy and there have been mistakes along the way. There will be more mistakes because Epstein does not walk on water and he is not without flaws.

But he has built a team that — on paper — is the best in the National League, and even if they don't win it all this year they will — barring extraordinary circumstances — have many chances over the next decade to win championships.

The tournament is unpredictable, but the more you get there, the more chances you have to win at least one.

For those still confused, that is the essence of the plan. ■

The Cubs formally introduced Theo Epstein as their new president of baseball operations on October 25, 2011. Since taking over, Epstein has built a winning team from the ground up through smart player development, key trades, and timely free-agent signings. (Photos by George Leclaire/Daily Herald)

CENTER FIELDER

24

DEXTER FOWLER

Cubs Have a Leadoff Leader in Fowler

By Bruce Miles, dailyherald.com | April 5, 2016

Chicago Cubs manager Joe Maddon has all kinds of lineup machinations and combinations at his disposal.

For the series finale against the Los Angeles Angels, Maddon switched things up against left-handed pitcher Andrew Heaney, getting right-handed batter Matt Szczur into the lineup in left field.

The middle of the order was different, too.

But there remains one constant: leadoff man Dexter Fowler.

When Fowler all but parachuted into spring training a few weeks back after his surprise re-signing with the Cubs, he solved a number of problems for the team. He plays a solid center fielder, and his return allowed Jason Heyward to

The surprise return of Dexter Fowler made an already formidable Cubs roster even better. (Steve Lundy/Daily Herald)

Above: Dexter Fowler returned to the Cubs lineup in late July after missing a month with a hamstring injury. (Mark Welsh/Daily Herald) Opposite: Dexter Fowler brings infectious energy and a team-first attitude to the top of the Cubs batting order. (Mark Welsh/Daily Herald)

move to his familiar spot in right.

And no matter what Maddon does in the middle and bottom of the batting order, Fowler is the guy at the top.

On Opening Night, Fowler went 3-for-4 with a walk and 3 runs scored. He made his presence felt immediately, leading off the game with a double and scoring.

"He's showed it last night; that's what he did pretty much the second half of last season," Maddon said Tuesday. "He was the guy who really got us going, and (Kyle) Schwarber hitting second. When Schwarbs came on line, it made a huge difference for us in the second half. It's set up a little bit differently now except for the fact that Dexter still is that guy."

It was a long winter of uncertainty for Fowler, who wound up coming back to the Cubs on a one-year deal (with a mutual option for 2017) on Feb. 25. A popular guy in the clubhouse, Fowler has slid right back into the fold.

"Team wise, yeah," he said. "We've got some unfinished business and are trying to take care of it this year."

Fowler put up a line of .250/.346/.411 last year with a career-best 17 home runs. Being the constant at the top of the order appeals to him.

"Oh, for sure," he said. "I've been hitting leadoff for my whole career — hitting first or second — so being out of the leadoff spot would definitely be change for me."

Maddon's catch phrase for Fowler when he goes to the plate is, "You go, we go." In other words, if Fowler is doing good things, the Cubs are enjoying success.

"Hopefully, that's not going away for several more years," Maddon said. "The ingratiating personality that he has and the energy that he has, all that stuff matters to us on a daily basis."

A switch hitter, Fowler batted .326 with 4 homers right-handed and .228 with 13 homers left-handed.

"It's always interesting to have him bat right-handed," Maddon said. "It's beautiful, man. The energy is great. Him showing up in camp and what he meant to the group is obvious. I feel pretty good about it." ■

OUTFIELDER / CATCHER

12

KYLE SCHWARBER

Cubs' Schwarber Can Learn a Lot During Rehab

By Dave Otto | April 9, 2016

Everyone associated with the Chicago Cubs has painted a positive and upbeat picture in response to Kyle Schwarber's season-ending injury. Based on last year's performance, and the additions of players such as Jason Heyward and Ben Zobrist, the Cubs appear to have some flexibility in their everyday lineup.

Joe Maddon did a great job last season of plugging players into different positions, and he will already be tested again this year. While this is a significant blow to the club, great clubs find a way to overcome it.

And now for Kyle. Hopefully, this will be the biggest obstacle that he has to overcome in his career. The rehab will be long and difficult. And it won't be easy for him to sit and watch his teammates compete. Kyle has indicated to the club that he wants to be with the team during his rehab

Despite a devastating, season-ending injury, Kyle Schwarber has plenty of opportunity to learn and grow as a young player.
(Steve Lundy/Daily Herald)

process, and that's outstanding to hear.

The beauty of baseball is you never stop learning. And while there is no substitute for being on the field and living it, there still is a lot to learn. I have heard many coaches (ex-players) say they wished they had coached before they played. Although impossible, I share those sentiments.

There are so many tidbits that you pick up while coaching and observing. You wish you could go back in time and apply those learning points to your own playing career.

While Kyle will not be a coach this season, he will have the opportunity to observe and learn from a little different perspective.

For example:
- Learn every pitcher in the league. Each pitcher has tendencies. One might tend to pitch backward, where he throws curveballs/change-ups when behind in the count (2 and 0), and fastballs when ahead in the count (1 and 2). One left-hander might try to pound the ball inside to left-handed power hitters with men on base. There might be an at-bat for Kyle in 2017 when that knowledge comes into play.

- Learn every hitter in the league. As a catcher, Kyle has double duty. Not only does he have to learn every pitcher in the league, but he has to figure out how to get hitters out. Every hitter has a hole in his swing, an area in the strike zone (or out of the zone) where you have a good chance of getting him out.

There is nothing more valuable to a pitcher than a catcher that is in sync with how you are trying to get hitters out. Kyle will have some time to spend with Cub pitchers and gain a greater understanding of how each pitcher works.

While rehabbing from his knee injury, Kyle Schwarber used the 2016 season as an opportunity to observe the National League's pitchers and catchers. (Joe Lewnard/Daily Herald)

Buster Posey of the San Francisco Giants suffered a season-ending injury on May 25, 2011. He was 24 years old at the time. The following year, Posey hit .336 and won the NL batting title. Posey and the Giants now have three World Series titles and I imagine Posey hasn't looked back.

Kyle Schwarber is 23 years old and had a nice start to his major-league career in 2015. Eventually Kyle will look back on 2016 as a bump in the road for him. It is now time for him to hammer his rehab and learn.

I have no doubt that he will. ■

Kyle Schwarber already has the skills to become one of the most exciting batters in the game. (John Starks/Daily Herald)

CHAMPIONSHIP DIGS

Players Love the New Clubhouse

By Bruce Miles, dailyherald.com | April 11, 2016

Cubs president Theo Epstein looked the part of the proud papa as he welcomed the Chicago Cubs and the media into the spacious new home clubhouse at Wrigley Field.

Actually, the Cubs got a first look at their new digs earlier after arriving in town from their road trip to Anaheim and Arizona.

The new locker room is the second-largest home clubhouse (the Yankees' is larger) in Major League Baseball, and it looks especially huge in contrast to the cramped quarters the Cubs occupied for many years.

"It was a lot of fun, to see the looks on their faces when they came in," Epstein said before the home opener. "Their faces lit up when they opened the doors and saw their new home.

"It's a special place. I've seen a lot of clubhouses. This is by far the nicest one I've ever seen."

For players such as Jason Heyward, Ben Zobrist and John Lackey, who joined the Cubs for the first time in the off-season, this is all they'll know as a home Cubs clubhouse. But for players such as first baseman Anthony Rizzo, a young veteran, it's a huge upgrade.

"It is really nice," Rizzo said. "It's going to be nice in the dog days, too. You can come in here and just relax."

The Cubs did get some initial walk-throughs during the January fan convention, when the clubhouse was still quite unfinished. But that,

Cubs players were dazzled by the sight of their new, upgraded clubhouse. (John Starks/Daily Herald)

along with the artist's renderings, prevented a total shock to the system.

"To see it live, we've seen all the demos and everything, but to see it live, it blew all our expectations away," Rizzo said.

In addition to the locker space, the new clubhouse, which is underground, features all new medical and training facilities. The old clubhouse now serves as a batting cage.

There's also a little "party room" to celebrate what the Cubs hope will be many victories.

"I think the clubhouse fits our identity as an organization and as a club pretty well. We believe in youth, young players. The clubhouse has kind of a young, energetic, fun feel to it. It also has everything you could ever need to improve yourself."

The clubhouse is part of the multiyear renovation of 102-year-old Wrigley Field. Epstein gave a nod toward team chairman Tom Ricketts.

"Tom did make the clubhouse a priority," Epstein said. ■

Above: The latest Wrigley Field renovations include new batting cages. (John Starks/Daily Herald) Opposite: The Cubs' new, much larger clubhouse features a "party room" for celebrations to come. (John Starks/Daily Herald)

JAKE THE GREAT

Arrieta Boggles the Mind with Another No-Hitter

By Bruce Miles, dailyherald.com | April 22, 2016

There's no way, right?

All the talk in spring training and throughout April was that Jake Arrieta could well have another great year for the Chicago Cubs, but there was no way he could put up the crazy kind of numbers he put up last year, especially in the second half.

You never want to say there's no way Arrieta could pitch a no-hitter so soon after last year's gem on Aug. 30 at Dodger Stadium, but his electric stuff makes that a possibility every time he takes the mound.

But no way, right?

Way.

So it was Thursday night at the Great American Ball Park in Cincinnati.

Maybe Arrieta had only his A-stuff instead of his A-plus-stuff, but he managed to no-hit the Cincinnati Reds in a game the Cubs won 16-0.

The 30-year-old Arrieta threw 119 pitches, walking four and striking out six.

"It felt sloppy from the get-go," Arrieta told TV broadcasters Len Kasper and Jim Deshaies on Comcast SportsNet. "The pregame (bullpen) was as

Jake Arrieta's second no-hitter in a Cubs uniform put him in elite company. (AP Images)

sloppy as it was in L.A. before that no-hitter. I don't put a lot into it. I was a little off with my command but I was able to keep them off-balance and later in the game pound the strike zone with some good movement and keep the ball down."

Here is how mind-boggling the numbers are for Arrieta:

- He went 22-6 with a 1.77 ERA last year, earning him the Cy Young Award. From the beginning of last year until now, Arrieta is 26-6 with an ERA of 1.66.

- Arrieta's last loss came last July 25, when the Phillies' Cole Hamels pitched a no-hitter against the Cubs at Wrigley Field.

- Going back to last year, Arrieta has a streak of 24 quality starts, a franchise record, and he has an ERA of 0.86 and a WHIP (walks plus hits per 1 inning pitched) of 0.70 in that streak.

- In his last 12 starts of last season, beginning Aug. 4, Arrieta was 11-0 with an ERA of 0.41. That is the lowest ERA for any pitcher from Aug. 1 until the end of the season since ERA became an official stat. Combine that with what Arrieta has done this year, and he is 15-0 with an ERA of 0.53.

- Arrieta became the third player in Cubs history to throw multiple no-hitters; Larry Corcoran had 3, and Ken Holtzman had 2, his second coming at Cincinnati. Arrieta is the first Cub to throw a no-hitter in back-to-back seasons. ■

Jake Arrieta's pitching repertoire has confused and frustrated batters across the league. (AP Images)

CLEAN SWEEP

Cubs Complete 'Crazy' Sweep with 13-Inning Win

By Bruce Miles, dailyherald.com | May 8, 2016

Baseball is the craziest, isn't it?

How else do you explain what happened on a sunny Mother's Day Sunday at Wrigley Field?

In a game the Cubs had no business winning in a lot of ways, they somehow pulled out a 4-3, 13-inning victory to complete a four-game sweep of the Washington Nationals and extend their overall winning streak to seven games.

Javier Baez hit a line-shot home run into the left-field bleachers against Blake Treinen with 1 out to cap this wild game.

"It's crazy, isn't it?" said Cubs manager Joe Maddon, whose team is 24-6. "The one thing that sums it up, and I mean this, and I have the privilege of being in our dugout: Our guys were in that game to the last drop. Long game like that and we're playing well, you could just mail it in. Our guys were into that game until the very last drop, I promise you that.

"To the last moment, everybody was there to win that game, and that's a beautiful thing."

Did we say this was crazy? Here's how crazy:

- For the second day in row, Maddon used all his bench players. With a partially depleted bullpen, he had to use reliever Trevor Cahill to bat. Cahill led off the bottom of the seventh inning with a single and later scored on Kris Bryant's 2-run single that tied the game at 3-3. Maddon also used a starting pitcher, Jason Hammel, to pinch hit.
- Cubs ace Jake Arrieta didn't have his best command and proved he was human, as he exited after only 5 innings with the Cubs down 3-1.
- Maddon topped even himself in the alchemy department by walking Nationals superstar Bryce Harper intentionally twice with runners on first and second. The move worked in

The Cubs used every tool and tactic available to them in an unforgettable win over the Washington Nationals. (AP Images)

the 10th inning, as the next hitter, Ryan Zimmerman, flied out. In the 12th, Zimmerman grounded out after the Cubs intentionally walked Harper with men on first and second.

On the day, Harper walked six times – tying a Major League record – with 3 being intentional. He also was hit by a pitch, giving him 7 plate appearances without an official at-bat. On Saturday, Harper came up 4 times without an at-bat.

"It's happened before to me; not at this level," Harper said of all the walks. "It was definitely when I was younger, in high school and college and whatnot. They had a plan. They had a plan and unfortunately it worked."

The plan was not to let the one man who could beat the Cubs do it.

"How good he is, if the other guy gets you, that's fine," Maddon said, referring to Zimmerman. "You have no problem with that whatsoever. I know that

Javier Baez's 13th inning home run was the deciding blow in a wild, hard-fought game. (AP Images)

he's not as hot as he can be coming into this series, but you don't want to get him hot. I've been part of that in the past. We did what we thought we had to do today, and it happened to work. So good for our guys."

Nationals manager Dusty Baker seemed chagrined, but he admitted it was probably the right thing to do.

"It might be, but the fans didn't come here to see him walk," Baker said. "They come to see him swing the bat."

In the early stages of this 4-hour, 54-minute day of wonderful baseball mess, Arrieta ran his pitch count to 100 over 5 innings. He gave up 6 hits and 3 runs (2 earned) while walking four, striking out seven and uncorking 3 wild pitches. He said he wasn't necessarily trying to put Harper on base aside from the fourth-inning intentional walk.

"I didn't command the ball really all that well, especially with my sinking fastball," he said. "I was erratic around the strike zone. There were times I tried to backdoor some off-speed to him, and I missed under the strike zone on the inner half of the plate, which made it hard for Tim (starting catcher Federowicz) to really handle those pitches.

"Commanding the ball today was a little off. He's a big weapon of theirs we obviously tried to neutralize throughout the series."

As for Baez, he entered as a pinch hitter in the eighth and stayed in at third base. He was going to be the emergency catcher if something happened to backup David Ross, who entered in the seventh.

Baez lined out to end the eighth with a man on base. His flyout in the 10th stranded a pair, but he found redemption with one swing of the bat in the 13th.

"I was just trying to get on base and get a good pitch to hit," he said. "That guy (Treinen) is throwing hard, 97 (mph) with sink. After the second strike, I just sat on the slider because they have been throwing it to me this series a lot. I was just looking for that pitch.

"The most important thing is that we never give up. We had nobody on the bench, and we were still playing hard and giving everything we have." ■

The Cubs' extra-inning victory was a Mother's Day treat and a testament to the persistence of this team. (AP Images)

CATCHER

DAVID ROSS

For Ross, Having Fun with Cubs Never Gets Old

By Bruce Miles, dailyherald.com | May 13, 2016

Everybody wants to talk about the kids on the Cubs.

But, hey, let's not forget the old man.

Catcher David Ross, who has turned into somewhat of a cult hero in what he says is his last season as a player, added to the legend in a 9-4 over the Pittsburgh Pirates at Wrigley Field. The victory snapped a mini two-game skid and moved the Cubs' record to 26-8.

It was the kids who got the Cubs started, with Addison Russell hitting a 3-run homer in the fourth inning and Kris Bryant igniting the 5-run fifth with a 2-run homer.

Ross added the cherry on top later that inning with a 3-run blast.

Speaking of that kind of stuff, it has been a party every day with Ross, who now has 99 home runs for his career. His teammates have been celebrating

Veteran catcher David Ross announced before the 2016 season that he would be retiring at season's end. The 39-year-old veteran saw more playing time than expected and caught his first career no-hitter and hit his 100th career home run during the first half. (Mark Welsh/Daily Herald)

with a countdown in the dugout.

"I am 39, that's all right," Ross said. "That's part of the reason why I'm having so much fun. I'm older. I can appreciate some things. When you have a group like this and you're part of it, when you've been around a little while and you see a special group, you should enjoy it. I try not to take that for granted because this is a really fun group."

Ross, a career backup thrust into heavy duty because of an injury to No. 1 catcher Miguel Montero, has been known for his defense more than his offense.

And that's rightly so, says manager Joe Maddon.

"The offense has been absolutely icing on the cake," Maddon said. "But this guy, he really is a field general when he's out there."

Ross and starting pitcher Jason Hammel worked well together as Hammel improved to 5-0 with a 1.77 ERA.

"Overall, I've just been competing," Hammel said. "Better strikes in the zone, I guess. Obviously having the curveball now — last year I was very sporadic with the curveball. I was a sinker-slider guy. If you can eliminate extra pitchers for a pitcher, it's an easier at-bat. Throwing the curveball for strikes, mix in a changeup here or there just to put it in the back of their head, then go with my bread and butter."

Hammel was asked how the Cubs would celebrate when Ross hits his 100th homer.

"Party favors, fireworks," he said. "It's going to be one heck of a celebration, though."

As Ross stood at his locker surrounded by reporters, his teammates gave him the good-natured business.

"Listen, if I don't get 100, it's not like I've had a terrible career," he said. "I am who I am. These guys are rooting for me to get 100 since I told them last year it's something I'd like to get, a nice even number, 100. It ain't like I'm going to go home and sulk. How about I'll hit 99 and we'll a World Series? That would make me just as happy as 100, that's for sure." ∎

Left: David Ross joined the Cubs before the 2015 season to back up Miguel Montero. (Joe Lewnard/Daily Herald) Opposite: David Ross warms up before a July 2016 game against the Brewers in Milwaukee. (Mark Welsh/Daily Herald)

LEADING TO THE TOP

Cubs' Clubhouse Not Lacking in Leaders

By Bruce Miles, dailyherald.com | May 21, 2016

Walk into the Chicago Cubs' sparkling new clubhouse and the first thing you notice is the shape: a perfect circle.

The diameter of that circle is 60 feet, 6 inches, meaning pitcher Jake Arrieta could warm up with catcher David Ross from across the room. The circle also means that no one locker is any more important than any other — neither status nor seniority gets rewarded with a prime slice of clubhouse real estate.

One thing you won't see on the crisp white uniforms hanging in those lockers is the letter "C" emblazoned on the front of any jersey to signify a team captain.

But what you will find are team leaders at any point along that circle: Arrieta as the ace of the pitching staff and example setter through his strenuous fitness regimen; Ross as the veteran vocal leader; Anthony Rizzo as the emerging young leader; Jon Lester as the veteran pitcher who now seems more comfortable in his own skin; and John Lackey as the guy who has helped Lester relax and brought a prickly presence to a young ballclub.

Each in his own way is a leader and a team captain without need of a letter to prove it. That's the way manager Joe Maddon likes it.

"I think it's an organic situation," said Maddon, who sprinkles the word "organic" liberally into his

Jake Arrieta greets his Cubs teammates after being introduced on Opening Day at Wrigley Field. The Cubs' ace leads by example through his strenuous fitness regimen. (John Starks/Daily Herald)

> **"If you're looking for labels around here to be 'the guy,' that's not the group we have in here. Everybody's 'the guy' in their own right. Everybody contributes in their own way."** —David Ross

conversations. "Leadership is taken. You can't give leadership. You can't give it to somebody. People have to take leadership. It's just the way it happens.

"You just can't anoint a leader. You can maybe through politics by having people vote for you, I guess. I've often thought that's a fabricated way of anointing a leader sometimes.

"But when you're within a group setting like this, with us there's no real hierarchy set up specifically. So if somebody wants to emerge as the leader, they have to take that. Players have to want to follow this particular person. I just can't say, 'Go put a C on your chest and all of a sudden people are going to listen to you.'"

Good Players and the Right Players

It goes without saying that good sports teams have talent, and the Cubs are a good team. The really great ones, the memorable ones, ooze an intangible quality that comprises confidence and accountability with just the right touch of fun loving.

Watching the movie, "Miracle," about the 1980 U.S. hockey team that won the Olympic gold medal, one can't help but be struck by the line uttered by coach Herb Brooks, portrayed by Kurt Russell.

When told by his assistant, Craig Patrick, that he was missing some of the best players, the Brooks character replies: "I'm not looking for the best players, Craig. I'm looking for the right ones."

There are obvious differences between amateur and professional teams, but it never hurts to have the right players in addition to a lot of very good ones.

The Cubs seem to believe they have both.

"I think it's a good mix," said Ross, a 39-year-old veteran who says this is his final season as a player. "Obviously, talent is No. 1. You've got to have good talent to win in the major leagues. You just can't bring in a bunch of good guys.

"You've got to bring in guys who want to be great and have the ability to be great and want to be great for the right reasons."

Cubs team president Theo Epstein built two world-championship teams in Boston, and he has turned the Cubs into contenders after overseeing three losing seasons from 2012-14. Last year's team advanced to the National League championship series, and the current squad has come out of the gate as the best team in the major leagues.

This past off-season, Epstein and general manager Jed Hoyer brought in free agents Jason Heyward, John Lackey and Ben Zobrist.

Heyward was the marquee signing, and he immediately drew a crowd of followers among teammates during spring training for his baseball acumen. Lackey is a plain-spoken Texan who isn't afraid to ruffle feathers. And Zobrist is known as being among the most solid citizens in the game.

"The longer I do this, the more I realize character really matters, makeup really matters," Epstein said. "Obviously you need talent, but the mix you have is really important. I think we have a really great clubhouse, a lot of quality individuals, so you want to add to that and enhance it. You don't want to do anything that might compromise it in any way.

"Zobrist is one of the many guys who makes your club that much better. He really cares about his teammates, sets a great example and is someone

Catcher David Ross emerged as a vocal veteran leader for the young, talented Cubs. (John Starks/Daily Herald)

you can sit down with and exchange ideas about baseball and life.

"He's been a great add to the clubhouse."

The edge Lackey brings also is important, according to Epstein.

"We have so many guys who are nice guys," he said. "We played hard (last year). We played intensely, but we transitioned from to a club that's in the crosshairs and has to show up every night over the course of 162 (games) to get where we want to go.

"Someone like Lackey demands excellence from his teammates. When he's on the mound, there's that little bit of extra gear. He holds everyone accountable. He's such a fierce competitor.

"It seems like a little added shot in the arm. And John's really well-liked by his teammates even though he does bring that edge every fifth day (on

the mound). That's something we didn't have in quite the same way. He adds to the mix without taking anything away from it at all."

Title for a Time Gone By

The Cubs have had team captains in the past. Late Hall of Famer Ron Santo captained the club from the mid-1960s until being traded to the White Sox after the 1973 season.

The title was revived in 2000, when manager Don Baylor bestowed it on pitchers Kevin Tapani and Rick Aguilera, first baseman Mark Grace and right fielder Sammy Sosa. Grace and Aguilera were gone after that season, so Baylor awarded the "C" to second baseman Eric Young and catcher Joe Girardi for 2001.

"To me, it's a responsibility," Baylor said in

Ben Zobrist, left, stands next to Javier Baez during batting practice. Zobrist, who played for Joe Maddon in Tampa Bay, emerged as a leader on and off the field. (Joe Lewnard/Daily Herald)

2000. "It's not just thrown out there. It means something."

The modern-day Cubs don't seem to be in any rush to formalize a captain's role.

"I think that's more different teams and tradition," Ross said. "If you're looking for labels around here to be 'the guy,' that's not the group we have in here. Everybody's 'the guy' in their own right. Everybody contributes in their own way.

"I think it's important about just knowing your role as a teammate and as a part of the club and doing your role to the best of your ability, whether that's to lead by example, to lead on the field, to lead the pitching staff, to be the second line on the pitching staff, whatever it is. Each person's role is important in its own right."

When Epstein was general manager of the Boston Red Sox, catcher Jason Varitek was the team captain. Epstein also sees no need to reprise the role with his Cubs of today.

"Personally, I don't think it's something that I ever set out to do and say, 'Hey, we should have a captain,'" he said. "If it gets to that point, it's probably too late. You probably don't have the right guys in there.

"But if somebody stands out as a clear, unquestioned leader or if somebody has been around a long time and might benefit in some way from a 'C' on his chest as a physical manifestation of what is already in place as far as a leadership dynamic, that might be something to consider. But that's not something I desire to do ever again."

As close as Maddon has come to the captain concept has been to meet with several players in spring training — players he termed "lead bulls" — to allow them to run with leadership responsibilities.

"When you are a good leader, you are really sensitive and have a lot of empathy toward everybody else around you," the manager said. "If you are looking for guys in clubhouses, I would look for empathy as much as anything regarding

Jake Arrieta stands on second base after hitting a double during a July game against the Mets. The 2015 National League Cy Young Award winner contributed with both his arm and his bat in 2016. (Joe Lewnard/Daily Herald)

whether or not you believe somebody's a leader. And also listening skills and somebody who is not always pontificating. That leads you in the wrong direction.

"I like the fact that it's spread out among them. The topic was leadership. I think that has to be taken more than it's being given." ■

SECOND BASEMAN / OUTFIELDER

18

BEN ZOBRIST

Hot-Hitting Zobrist Brings Critical Leadership

By Jordan Bernfield | May 29, 2016

Jason Heyward grabbed more offseason headlines, but another free agent acquisition has made a much greater impact for the Cubs this year.

He's a career .268 hitter with a .358 on-base percentage, but through Sunday's action he has the highest on-base percentage .451 and the second-highest batting average .351 in baseball.

Ben Zobrist has been one of the Cubs' most valuable players, ranking 3rd on the team in WAR 2.3. And right now, he's red hot.

"Zo's been unbelievable," the Cubs' manager said on the "Spiegel and Goff Show" on WSCR-AM 670. "He's been so consistent. You can hit him anywhere in the top five numbers, and he's going to give you a great at-bat, not a good at-bat."

After easing into things with his new team through April, Zobrist is batting a sizzling .422 in May, with a whopping .505 on-base percentage. He has been almost equally prolific from both sides of

Switch-hitting utility man Ben Zobrist joined the Cubs in 2016 after 10 years in the American League with Tampa Bay, Oakland and Kansas City. (Mark Welsh/Daily Herald)

the plate, though he has had far fewer at-bats right-handed.

More notably, he's putting up these numbers while posting the lowest swing-rate in baseball this season, per Fangraphs.com. On a team built to wear pitchers down with lengthy at-bats, Zobrist provides the Cubs quality plate appearances virtually every time, regardless of result. He swings when he gets a pitch to drive, and takes when he doesn't. It seems simple, but it's one of the hardest skills for hitters to master.

What a great example he provides his young teammates still forming their offensive identities in the big leagues.

Though the Cubs are defined by their surplus of young talent, veterans like Zobrist provide critical leadership skills and invaluable experience to teams with championship aspirations. That's why President Theo Epstein spent $56 million for four years of Zobrist, who turned 35 this past Thursday. While he's not likely to maintain this pace, Joe Maddon isn't surprised by the steady presence his versatile 2nd baseman provides.

Zobrist began his big league career in Tampa Bay, playing nine seasons for Maddon on a young team that turned the Rays' franchise from a perennial doormat into an American League power. Maddon made him into baseball's "super-utility" player, providing good defense at numerous positions while also hitting proficiently from both sides of the plate.

Last year, Zobrist was traded midseason from Oakland to the Royals and played a key role in leading Kansas City to its first World Series title since 1985.

Now in his second tour with Maddon, Zobrist is a perfect fit both on the field and in the clubhouse for a young team ready to win. He's one of the players entrusted to show the young guys both how to approach their daily work and how to handle high-pressure situations come October.

The Cubs signed Ben Zobrist to a four-year, $56 million contract after the 2015 season. (Mark Welsh/Daily Herald)

Earlier this season, Royals' General Manager Dayton Moore drove from Kansas City to meet the Cubs in St. Louis, where they were playing the Cardinals. He hand-delivered Zobrist his World Series ring from last year. Zobrist's young teammates loved it — especially Anthony Rizzo, who wore it around the clubhouse.

"We're in the middle of trying to win one here in Chicago," Zobrist said. ■

After moving between the infield and outfield most of his career, Zobrist played primarily at second base during the first half of the 2016 season. (Mark Welsh/Daily Herald)

RELIEF PITCHER

37

TRAVIS WOOD

Wood Steps Up Big for Cubs

By Bruce Miles, dailyherald.com | May 30, 2016

Chicago Cubs manager Joe Maddon could not stop talking about relief pitcher Travis Wood after a 2-0 victory over the Los Angeles Dodgers at Wrigley Field. Could. Not. Stop. Talking.

As soon as Maddon hit the interview room for the postgame session, he said: "You really should be talking to Travis."

Soon enough.

Partway through his interview, Maddon simply summed up the day's proceedings: "I think it's truly Travis Wood's day. He set that whole game up, period."

Wood, a left-hander, found himself pressed into emergency relief duty at the start of the third inning when starter Jason Hammel went to the ground with cramping in his right hamstring. Hammel received attention from the athletic trainer but could not go after he had pitched 2 innings, giving up 1 hit.

There would be no more hits for the Dodgers on this day, when the Cubs won their sixth in a row to improve to 35-14.

Wood came in and worked 4 perfect innings to get the victory. He was followed by Justin Grimm, Pedro Strop and Hector Rondon, who

The Cubs' longest tenured player, left-hander Travis Wood emerged as a key late-inning contributor out of the bullpen in 2016.
(Joe Lewnard/Daily Herald)

After being used exclusively as a starter during his first three seasons with the Cubs, Travis Wood moved to the bullpen in 2015. (Mark Welsh/Daily Herald)

earned his ninth save.

Wood was entitled to as much time as he needed to warm up after Hammel's injury, but he got ready quickly.

"I did feel good," he said. "I made a few more pitches than normal just to get loose because I didn't get fully loose. But I'm not going to make the game wait for me to get loose. Once I feel I can execute pitches, it's time to go."

The 29-year-old Wood is one of the quiet success stories on the Cubs over the past year. He lost his starting job early last season but has redefined himself as a reliever to be used in any situation. He says there's a certain pride he takes in that.

"Absolutely," he said. "Going to the bullpen and everything, but when they call your name, it's still pitching. Go out there and make your pitches. Get the guys out, and help your team in any way you can."

Once he got rolling against the Dodgers, Wood was super efficient, throwing 43 pitches, 35 for strikes.

As for Hammel, he expressed optimism that the injury was "just a cramp" that would not cost him time. He was able to joke about his contribution to the game.

"I blew the no-hitter," he said. "It makes me feel real small. I obviously wanted to stay in there. It (stinks), something like that, where it's on and off. After I stretched it and I was down on the ground, I threw the first (warmup) pitch, it was fine.

"I threw the next pitch, and it (the cramping) was back. It would have taken us six hours to get through the game if I had stayed in there."

The Dodgers' only hit came with two outs in the first. Justin Turner singled on a little flyball to right center that dropped as center fielder Jason Heyward, right fielder Ben Zobrist and second baseman Javier Baez gave chase. Heyward was in center because Dexter Fowler was out of the lineup with a sore heel, forcing Heyward to move over from right.

The Cubs scored both of their runs in the fifth with the help of some poor Dodgers defense. Zobrist led off with a single, and when right fielder Yasiel Puig misplayed the ball for an error, Zobrist raced to third base. He also extended a hitting streak to 16 games, tying a career high.

Heyward drove Zobrist home on an infield single to first baseman Adrian Gonzalez, who had nowhere to go with the ball. After Kris Bryant struck out, Anthony Rizzo doubled home Heyward.

But the man of the moment on this gorgeous Memorial Day was Wood.

"The bullpen in general, but Travis for sure," catcher David Ross said. "Those guys get loose a little bit later, and he had to rush and get out there.

"Credit to him. He's always had a good rubber arm since I've known him. He can pitch on short rest. Even when he was a starter, he would go long in a game, deep into games when he had his good stuff. All those guys are impressive, but Woody continues to impress me about how professional he is on a daily basis." ■

IMPACT D

Baez and Teammates Spearhead Overlooked Defense

By Dave Otto | June 11, 2016

Considering the Cubs are winning twice as many games as they are losing, there are many elements to their game that are going well.

Cubs starting pitchers have taken their team deep into games on most nights. Conversely, the Cubs offense has managed to get into the other team's bullpens early. No matter how good the Cubs are swinging the bats though, if they run into a string of starters that are throwing the ball well, runs can be tough to come by. In those games — dare I say playoff games — the spotlight shifts to the defense.

Over the last couple of years, this Cubs franchise has found and developed players that are as good at flashing that leather as they are at swinging the bat.

At third base, Kris Bryant might be the most accurate thrower in the league. Last year, a couple of balls would sail on him when throwing across the diamond. By getting his feet in a better position and his arm up this year when making a throw, he has become more consistent.

Addison Russell has tremendous range at short and will make the occasional error simply because he gets to more balls than others. He too, runs into the occasional problem of throwing to first when his arm drops and the ball sails on him.

Ben Zobrist has yet to make an error this year.

Anthony Rizzo is a big target for infielders over at first and has developed into one of the better first basemen in the league.

What a luxury for manager Joe Maddon to plug in Javier Baez at every infield position. Rarely does a team have a super-utility player like Baez where you don't miss a beat wherever you put him on the diamond.

From the vantage point of the broadcast booth, there were some Cubs teams in the past that looked slow in the outfield compared to their opponents,

Second baseman Javier Baez tags out Rougned Odor during a July 2016 game against the Texas Rangers. Baez provided plus defense at all four infield positions in 2016. (Joe Lewnard/Daily Herald)

particularly in the bigger ballparks around the league like Colorado and Pittsburgh (left-center gap). That is no longer the case with Jason Heyward and Dexter Fowler getting consistent great jumps on balls hit their way.

While there is not as much room to cover at Wrigley Field, it does pose that one big challenge: There's no padding behind that ivy-covered wall. Only brick, and outfielders are reluctant getting to that brick at the same time that the ball does. Because of that, outfielders tend to play a little bit deeper to ensure they can find the wall first, instead of banging into it.

Dexter Fowler apparently is playing hitters a little bit deeper this year. Sure, there might be an occasional hit that now dumps in on him in shallow center. By playing deeper, though, he is able to find the wall easier on balls hit over his head, and he has taken away many doubles and triples.

Recent call-up and prospect Albert Almora has already made an impact by throwing a runner out at home plate in Philly, and making a sliding catch in Atlanta.

Typically, a ground ball that an infielder either boots or can't get to costs a team one out and runners might only advance one base. An error or a missed attempt on a ball in the outfield might cost a team one out and two or three bases. In mid-June, this Cubs pitching staff is talented enough to pitch over the occasional error or missed attempt in a 5-run game. In October baseball however, every out and every base takes on greater significance. The game changes, and this Cubs defense sure looks built for that possibility. ∎

CONTRERAS AND ALMORA TAKE THE BIG STAGE

Cubs' Moves Bring Team Competition

By Dave Otto | June 18, 2016

The late, great Satchel Paige was once quoted as saying, "Don't look back, something might be gaining on you." While it is unclear in what context the Hall of Famer was quoted, those words ring true with this Cubs team and some of their recent roster moves.

The Cubs organization has a farm system so rich in talent that most of their call-ups have hit the ground running.

For individual players, there will always be that player right around the corner looking to take your job. With the recent call-ups of outfielder Albert Almora and catcher Willson Contreras, the Cubs organization continues to crank out the players.

Trades and call-ups ultimately will affect playing time for those currently playing certain positions. Currently for the Cubs, the battle for playing time resides in the outfield and behind the plate. Under the right circumstances and with the right type of players, that competition of someone gaining on you can be great for a team.

For an individual player, instead of looking back, he needs to just be ready when his name is called to do something on the field. Matt Szczur only had 6 at-bats on the recent road trip. Joe Maddon batted Szczur second against the Pirates, and what does he do? He hits a 2-run home run in the first inning to get the Cubs going. He's fighting for playing time, and he is getting it done.

Almora is pushing to stay in the big leagues. With a game-winning hit against the Washington Nationals, and some sparkling plays in the outfield, he has taken advantage of his opportunity so far.

It sounds like the Cubs intend to have Contreras up for a short time, primarily to get a taste of the big leagues. There is so much that goes into the catching position, that every day in the majors will be valuable to Contreras in learning the pitching staff.

Each pitcher has their own quirks on how they like to work with their catcher. Some pitchers like their catcher to give their target early even before starting their pitching motion. While others prefer their catcher to set up their target a little bit later when they are actually in their motion to the plate.

Some pitchers, like Jon Lester, prefer their catcher to move their entire body for a target when throwing to the outside corner of the plate. Others prefer their catcher to set up down the middle with their body, and just move their glove. Coming into a game one time, I had a catcher ask me on the mound what my name was. There's no excuse for giving up 2 home runs that day, but I sure wish he would've asked me instead how I like my target.

Either by observing games at the big-league level, or by actually calling a few games, this gives Contreras the opportunity to get acclimated real quick. This Cubs staff has been really good so far, and if Jake Arrieta likes his coffee with cream and sugar, I would make note of that.

There is no secret here, Contreras could eventually start pushing Miguel Montero and David Ross for playing time behind the plate. Yet Montero and Ross will do everything they possibly can do to get Contreras ready to handle this staff. Contreras is a right-handed hitter that could give Joe Maddon another vital option against left-handed pitching, or a team with a good running game.

While there is always that fight for playing time on a team, what's unique about this Cubs team is that ultimately it is all about winning. Just be ready. ■

Top: Catcher Willson Contreras made his major league debut in June 2016. (Joe Lewnard/Daily Herald) Bottom: Albert Almora makes a diving catch to rob Texas' Ryan Rua of an extra-base hit during a July game. (Joe Lewnard/Daily Herald)

BRYANT HITS IT BIG

Historic Night for Bryant Lifts Arrieta to 12th Win

By Bruce Miles, dailyherald.com | June 28, 2016

When Kris Bryant reached the dugout after his record-setting third home run, thousands of Cubs fans in the stands cheered for a curtain call. A few teammates wanted him to take a bow, too.

Nope. That was the only thing the Cubs' top hitter wouldn't do on his historic night.

Bryant became the first major-leaguer to hit 3 home runs and 2 doubles in a game, and Jake Arrieta added a solo shot in the ballpark where he threw a no-hitter in April, leading the Cubs to an 11-8 victory over the Cincinnati Reds on Monday night.

"The last couple of weeks haven't been what I've wanted, so I figured I'm due," said Bryant, who hit 3 homers one time during a college game with San Diego.

Arrieta (12-2) threw his second career no-hitter April 21 in a 16-0 win over the Reds. Bryant led the way with a pair of homers in that game, including a grand slam that gave him a career-high 6 RBI.

Arrieta struggled in his return to Cincinnati, giving up a season-high 5 runs in 5 innings, but

Kris Bryant celebrates with Jake Arrieta after homering in the fourth inning of the Cubs' June 27 win in Cincinnati. Bryant became the first major-leaguer to hit 3 home runs and 2 doubles in a game. (AP Images)

Bryant drove in 6 runs again to help the right-hander pull through. Bryant's 16 total bases were a Cubs record (topping the old mark by 2), and his 5 hits marked a career high.

"That keeps you back from those 0-for-20 stretches when you have a game like this," Bryant said.

Most of the 31,762 fans wore Cubs blue and demanded a curtain call after the third homer. Bryant wouldn't oblige, considering it inappropriate on the road.

"He enjoys the moment, but he doesn't go over the top with it," Cubs manager Joe Maddon said. "He's very old school. He doesn't spike the ball in the end zone. He just lays it down or hands it to the official."

The Cubs improved to 49-26 for the season, while Arrieta upped his own mark to 12-2 with an ERA of 2.10 (up from 1.74) and a WHIP of 1.02 as he pitched 5 innings, walking five and striking out four.

Arrieta has started 12 games since his no-hitter, going 8-2 with an ERA of 2.63 and a WHIP of 1.17. The ERA and WHIP numbers are slightly above his season marks, but hardly terrible.

If anything, Arrieta and the Cubs have been lamenting that other teams have been making him work hard to get the outs.

That was the case again Monday. The Cubs scored 2 runs in the first inning, 1 on an RBI double by Bryant and the other on a sacrifice fly by Miguel Montero.

But the Reds tied it in the home half, as Arrieta threw 27 pitches. A quick 1-2-3 second was followed by a 22-pitch third, when the Reds tied the game at 3-3 after Bryant's solo homer in the top of the inning.

The Cubs looked to be sitting pretty after they scored 4 runs in the fourth, the big blow being Bryant's 3-run homer, a 444-foot monster shot to left.

Arrieta gave himself an 8-3 lead with his home run but found trouble in the bottom of the fifth when Joey Votto hit a 2-run homer. Pitching coach Chris Bosio visited Arrieta in the inning, and left-hander Travis Wood was warming up in the bullpen.

Arrieta averted further trouble, but he did run his pitch count to 93, and Maddon went to Trevor Cahill in the sixth.

A look at the numbers shows no big differences for Arrieta except for the walk rates, suggesting a lack of command on some days. His walks-per-9-innings has gone from 1.89 to 3.21 (entering Monday) and his strikeouts-to-walks ratio was down from 4.92 to 3.06 while his walks percentage rose from 5.5 to 9.1.

As for Bryant, he also is the first player in Cubs history to have 5 extra-base hits in a game.

He became the third major-leaguer since 1900 to have at least 3 homers and a total of 5 extra-base hits. Josh Hamilton had 4 homers and a double in 2012, and Joe Adcock had 4 homers and a double in 1954, per Elias Sports Bureau research provided by the Reds.

Before Bryant, the last Cubs player with 3 homers in a game was Dioner Navarro, on May 29, 2013, against the White Sox. ∎

Kris Bryant's 3-homer, 2-double game against the Reds helped the Cubs improve their record to 49–26 through 75 games. (AP Images)

ALL-STAR GAME BOUND

Cubs Make History with 7 All-Star Selections

By Bruce Miles, dailyherald.com | July 6, 2016

If you're going to send seven players to the All-Star Game, you might as well make a little history.

The Chicago Cubs did that Tuesday, as they placed seven on the roster for next Tuesday's All-Star Game at San Diego.

Their entire infield will go as starters: first baseman Anthony Rizzo, second baseman Ben Zobrist, third baseman Kris Bryant and shortstop Addison Russell.

The only time one team's infield started a Midsummer Classic was 1963, when the St. Louis Cardinals sent Bill White, Julian Javier, Ken Boyer and Dick Groat. Second baseman Javier was a sub for the injured Bill Mazeroski of the Pirates.

In addition to the infield, other Cubs going to San Diego are center fielder Dexter Fowler and pitchers Jake Arrieta and Jon Lester.

Rizzo is the first Cub to lead the NL in fan voting since Derrek Lee in 2005. The Cubs have never had five players named to start the All-Star Game and are the first team to do so since the 1985 San Diego Padres. This is the biggest Cubs contingent to make the all-star team since eight were named in 2008.

"It means a lot," said the 22-year-old Russell, making his first all-star appearance. "Ever since I was a little kid, that's all I wanted to do, was make the All-Star Game. Just to be able to do that in a short amount of time that I have in the big leagues

Seven Cubs made the 2016 National League All-Star roster — clockwise: Jake Arrieta, Dexter Fowler, Anthony Rizzo, Kris Bryant, Addison Russell, Jon Lester and Ben Zobrist. (Daily Herald Staff Photos)

makes it a little bit better. Hopefully it's the first of a few."

It's also the first All-Star Game for Arrieta, who won the Cy Young Award last year and just may find himself the starting pitcher in the Midsummer Classic.

"There you go," he said. "I think it's up for grabs, maybe. I think there are several guys that could be deserving of starting the game, whether it's me or not. It's not a huge deal one way or another. It would be great to start. It would also be great to pitch in the game, just to be a part of the three days or so in San Diego. Either way they go, it's still going to be a really good experience for all of us."

Arrieta was chosen by the players while Lester was chosen by NL manager Terry Collins. This is Lester's fourth all-star team but his first in the National League.

Fowler is on the disabled list, but he's hoping his hamstring heals in time for him to play in his first All-Star Game.

"Yeah, it's awesome," said Fowler, who didn't have a team all winter until re-signing with the Cubs early in spring training. "Definitely a blessing. I worked hard this off-season and endured a lot this off-season. Fortunately I came back here and had the start I did."

Zobrist, a two-time American League all-star, gave a tip of the cap to Cubs fans, who got out the vote.

That's cool," he said. "I think what that says is we have an incredible fan base that's in our corner as players. For that, we become the (beneficiaries). That's why people want to play for the Cubs.

"Sure, there are plenty of guys who have earned that, who don't have those same votes. I think for that fact, we're glad we're Chicago Cubs right now. That's why a lot of players really want to be here."

Bryant and Rizzo went together as the Cubs' all-star representatives last year. Bryant, an MVP candidate this year with 25 homers, was a rookie last season. Rizzo will be making his third all-star appearance.

"Last year, I didn't even think was going to go, just because it was my first year," Bryant said. "Everything was going crazy. Looking back on it, it was an awesome time. It's an honor. To have a lot of my teammates there with me would make it even more fun. It's a huge honor to be an all-star. It's hard to put into words how cool the All-Star Game was last year."

Rizzo echoed that.

"It's fun," he said. "It's where you want to be every single year."

Manager Joe Maddon lauded his players and the organization.

"I think it means a lot," he said. "First of all, individually, I've talked about it before, what it does for your own personal self-esteem is very valuable. There's a lot of fan acceptance within that. There's some peer acceptance within that. You've wanted to play since you're a kid. You're an all-star, man. That's pretty sweet stuff.

"Organizationally, it just speaks to what's been done here the last several years. I've been talking about that. I take zero credit for that. It's just great."

Of course, the Cubs may have some extra incentive to do well in the All-Star Game as the winning league gets home-field advantage in the World Series. Of course, the Cubs have to get there first in October.

"I don't have any strong opinions one way or the other, I really don't," Maddon said on the game determining home field. "The only fact that I do like about it is that it makes the game actually more competitive. I think that sets our All-Star Game apart from, like, a Pro Bowl or an NBA All-Star Game." ■

Anthony Rizzo was the leading vote-getter for the 2016 All-Star Game in San Diego. (Joe Lewnard/Daily Herald)

THIRD BASEMAN / OUTFIELDER

KRIS BRYANT

Bryant Has What it Takes to Be MVP

By Jordan Bernfield | July 9, 2016

After the first half of the baseball season, Cubs' All-Star Kris Bryant is the Most Valuable Player in the National League. He is one of baseball's most prolific hitters this season, with the highest Fangraphs WAR, most home runs, highest on-base percentage, and second-most RBI in the National League. He has also played above-average defense in the infield and outfield at six different positions this season, and has started at four.

The MVP award is often given to the offensive player of the year. Defense typically takes a back seat to the player's offensive contributions. If Bryant remains one of the NL's best hitters in the second half of the season, his abilities with his many gloves should be the deciding factor for the award.

Rarely does a player of Bryant's offensive caliber show defensive versatility like the Cubs' slugger. Should Bryant win the National League MVP this year, he'd be the first winner since Johnny Bench in 1972 to appear at as many as four positions in a season. Bench served primarily as the Reds' catcher, but also made ten starts in right field, four at third base, and two at first base.

Kris Bryant is a serious candidate to be the Cubs' first National League MVP since Sammy Sosa in 1998. (Mark Welsh/Daily Herald)

Bryant has made 47 starts at 3rd base, 26 in left field, nine in right field, three at 1st base, and has played an inning each in center field and at shortstop. His combined 1.2 defensive WAR at 3rd base and left field is more than serviceable.

In fact, Bryant has only started at his natural position, 3rd base, 57-percent of the time. Of the top ten players in offensive WAR this season per Fangraphs (Bryant ranks 3rd overall, 1st in the NL), just the Orioles' Manny Machado and the Rangers' Ian Desmond have started at their natural positions less frequently. Machado has played 3rd base 45-percent of the time, and Desmond signed with the Rangers knowing he would be converted from an infielder to an outfielder this season.

Besides Bryant, only the Astros' Jose Altuve, Machado, and Desmond have played more than one defensive position. While Machado regularly switches between shortstop and 3rd base, and Desmond alternates between left and center field,

Altuve has played all but one game at 2nd base.

And remember, Machado, Desmond and Altuve all play in the American League, making Bryant by far the most versatile elite offensive player in the National League. The only other National Leaguers in the top ten in offensive WAR — Dodgers' shortstop Corey Seager and Diamondbacks' 3rd baseman Jake Lamb — have not changed positions this season.

Bryant is on pace to hit 48 home runs. That would be the most by a Cubs player since Derrek Lee swatted 46 in 2005. It would also be the most by a National League player since Albert Pujols smashed 47 round-trippers in 2009.

Neither of those guys played anywhere but first base. Bryant manned first base this year, but more regularly 3rd base, left field, and right field. If it comes down to a comparison of statistics between Bryant and another hitter, the Cubs' all-star's versatility should give him the edge. ■

Above: Kris Bryant had 25 home runs heading into the All-Star break. (Joe Lewnard/Daily Herald) Opposite: Kris Bryant's defensive versatility has provided flexibility for Cubs manager Joe Maddon. During the first half, Bryant started games at third base, left field, right field and first base. (Joe Lewnard/Daily Herald)

STARTING PITCHER

28

KYLE HENDRICKS

Cubs Have Something Special in Hendricks

By Dave Otto | July 16, 2016

With 8 wins and an ERA of 2.41, Kyle Hendricks is putting together quite a year for the Cubs. Against the Texas Rangers on Friday, Hendricks kicked off the Cubs' second half with 6 innings of scoreless work against one of the better offenses in the American League. Joe Maddon alluded to just how good Hendricks has been by indicating in Friday's post-game conference that he has been one of the better pitchers in the National League.

Hendricks does not throw 95 mph and he does not have a nasty cutter or breaking ball. However, what he does have is a sinking fastball that looks like it falls off a table and a changeup that puts the brakes on halfway to home plate. His arsenal of stuff is different, which makes it refreshing to see that pitchers can thrive without throwing 94 mph.

There are so many pitchers in today's game that throw gas.

Kyle Hendricks emerged as one of the National League's top pitchers during his second full major league season. (Mark Welsh/Daily Herald)

The Cleveland Indians used to have a radar gun in their dugout at old Municipal Stadium in the early 90s. I only saw two starting pitchers throw consistently above 90 mph, Roger Clemens and Bret Saberhagen.

While radar guns have changed, and readings might be a little juiced up, pitchers just throw harder now. With all this velocity, the pendulum has swung a little more in the pitchers favor.

Yet today's hitters are that much quicker and stronger, too. They can catch up to that 95 mph heater. And the more a hitter sees 95 mph, the more likely he is to get adjusted to that kind of velocity. Facing Hendricks, hitters have to adjust the other way. They are just not used to facing an 88 mph fastball with that much sink.

Hendricks doesn't throw a sinker. He throws something different, a "turbo" sinker. Cubs catcher Willson Contreras boxed or mishandled a couple of

pitches that Hendricks threw on Friday. In defense of Contreras, this is a whole new staff that he has to get accustomed to, and he will only get better with time. Contreras' struggle to catch or frame a few of Hendricks' pitches does indicate just how much late movement Hendricks has on his pitches.

As long as it doesn't lead to runs, I imagine it has be a pretty good feeling for Hendricks, or any other pitcher, when a catcher struggles on a few pitches. It sure beats the alternative. Former catcher and Cubs coach Matt Sinatro once asked me if he needed to use his glove in catching me, or could he just use a pair of tweezers.

Hendricks' challenges are similar to what every other pitcher encounters in a league of really good hitters. The more times a hitter sees him, the more comfortable hitters will be with adjustments.

The Rangers on Friday, had never faced Hendricks and it was evident. There were some funny swings at some pitches and they chased others out of the zone.

Over time hitters will try and lay off swinging at his sinking fastball down. And if Hendricks isn't getting strike calls on those pitches down in the zone, he will have to try and elevate his sinker. High sinkers tend to get hit a long way and that's where he will have to continue to keep hitter's off-balance with his change-up.

Hendricks' demeanor on the mound is close to stoic. It's difficult to tell by looking at him on the mound whether he is up 5 runs, or down 5. The "turbo" sinker and changeup require some touch and the calm, aggressive approach appears to be working well for him.

There will be games where that touch will not be there. But overall, Hendricks' has something that is different, and that is a big plus for the Cubs. ■

Left: Kyle Hendricks was acquired from the Texas Rangers at the trade deadline in 2012 in a trade for pitcher Ryan Dempster. (Joe Lewnard/Daily Herald) Opposite: Kyle Hendricks' calm, aggressive approach has led to a breakout season in 2016. (Joe Lewnard/Daily Herald)

NEW YORK NIXED

Chicago Cubs Finally Get One Against Mets

By Bruce Miles, dailyherald.com | July 19, 2016

Chicago Cubs vs. New York Mets used to be a thing, back in the day, when both were part of the National League East.

The rivalry died down some when the Mets stayed in the East and the Cubs moved to the Central.

But last year's National League championship series — won by the Mets over the Cubs in a four-game sweep — put the Big Apple-Second City rivalry back into the forefront.

The Mets came to town Monday night having swept the Cubs in four more recently at Citi Field in New York.

The Cubs righted things for themselves, at least for Monday night, with a 5-1 victory at Wrigley Field.

Jon Lester worked 7⅔ innings of 4-hit, 1-run ball, and Anthony Rizzo staked Lester to a 3-0 lead with a 3-run homer to right-center in the third inning. It was Rizzo's 22nd homer of the season.

Whether the Cubs were "up" or needed to be "up" for this series is a matter of debate.

Manager Joe Maddon isn't one to go that route, saying no one game is any more important than another. But Lester said he liked the way the Cubs played in this one.

"I think that's the biggest thing; we didn't play very well in New York," said Lester, who is 10-4 with a 2.89 ERA. "We came out tonight and played clean baseball. We had really good quality at-bats

Anthony Rizzo watches a home run sail into the right field seats during the Cubs' 5-1 win over the Mets on July 18.

(Mark Welsh/Daily Herald)

… That's really big for us, especially when young guys start doing that.

"Like I said, tonight we played really, really good defense on the left side, all over. I think that's the key for us, just getting back to clean baseball with these guys."

Rizzo put a textbook at-bat together against Mets lefty Steven Matz, fouling off pitch after pitch in the third inning before rocketing a ball into the bleachers in right-center for his 22nd homer of the season. The home run came on the 10th pitch of the at-bat.

As far as the Cubs' offense goes, Maddon called Rizzo "the anchor of the whole thing."

"Matz has good stuff; he's tough on lefties," Rizzo said. "Just battle there. Fight, fight some tough pitches off. I put a good swing on one he left over the plate."

Like Lester, Rizzo said it was good to beat the Mets after what happened last fall and just a few games ago.

"Yeah, we just got done with Texas," Rizzo said of the Cubs beating the Rangers two of three over the weekend. "They're a good team. The Mets are a good team. To take the first game of the series, we've got Jake (staff ace Arrieta) going tomorrow. See what happens."

Maddon could not stop talking about Rizzo's homer.

"Don't underestimate what a great at-bat by Rizzo," said Maddon, whose team is 56-36. "That's is a fabulous at-bat. That's what you're looking for. Not everybody will hit a home run, but to really grind out an at-bat, foul pitches off with two strikes, get to the next pitch, get to the next pitch." ∎

Above: Cubs shortstop Addison Russell blasts a double in the bottom of the first inning against the Mets. (Mark Welsh/Daily Herald) Opposite: Cubs fan Tristan Rackow of Western Springs flies the W flag after the Cubs' win over the Mets. (Mark Welsh/Daily Herald)

GAME CHANGER

Chapman Powers His Way Onto Scene for Cubs

By Bruce Miles, dailyherald.com | July 28, 2016

The save situation had gone by the wayside, but the Wrigley Field crowd got what it came for anyway.

It was almost like the band coming back on stage for an encore when Aroldis Chapman entered the game. The Chicago Cubs had just busted open a 3-1 game in the bottom of the eighth inning with 5 runs against the Chicago White Sox.

As they were doing that, Chapman was warming up for a possible save.

He came on anyway and closed out the 8-1 victory, and it was a show in and of itself.

With every fastball that hissed up to the plate at 101, 102, 103 mph, the crowd of 41,166 gasped as the triple-digit velocity figure was posted on the videoboard in left field.

Just for fun, Chapman threw a slider – a slider – at 91 mph to strike out Jose Abreu leading off. He then dispatched Todd Frazier on a groundout and Avisail Garcia on a called third strike.

Game over. Game changer for the Cubs, who now have a closer who can do freakishly unfair things with a baseball.

It was a reluctant Chapman who talked to the media afterward, getting interpreting help from Cubs catcher Miguel Montero.

"The adrenaline was pretty good even though it wasn't a save situation," Chapman said through Montero. "It was fun to hear the crowd cheer for me."

In the Cubs' dugout, manager Joe Maddon played the scoreboard-watching game right along with the crowd.

"It's just entertaining to watch the (radar) gun, beyond everything else," Maddon said. "Of course, you're looking to get the win. It's different. He's a different kind of a pitcher. You don't see that, every 100 years or so. He's just that good. Everybody talks about the fastball. How good is the slider? The slider is devastating.

Aroldis Chapman's fastball has been clocked at speeds up to 105 mph. (Joe Lewnard/Daily Herald)

"It was very cool. I've seen it on the wrong side. It's nice to have it on your side. Give the guy some credit for going out there in somewhat of a difficult situation based on the last couple days. I don't even know how much rest he's gotten."

Of course, there's always one guy to spoil the party.

"I'm not impressed," said starting pitcher Jason Hammel. "I thought we were getting a guy who threw 105 (mph)."

Hammel was just kidding. But there's no fooling as to what the addition of Chapman could mean to the Cubs as they pursue a World Series title.

He is as close as there is to a lockdown closer, and that's allowing the Cubs to use former closer Hector Rondon in the eighth. Rondon went 1-2-3 on the night.

The Cubs picked up Chapman in a trade with the New York Yankees. After two days of discussion about Chapman's suspension this year for violating Major League Baseball's policy on domestic violence, it was back to baseball.

At first, Chapman did not wish to speak with the Chicago media after the game, but he relented and seemed happy enough about the game.

"Obviously, the crowd kind of pumped me up a little bit," he said. "I was excited because it was my debut with (the Cubs)."

If he reached "only" 103 mph because the adrenaline wasn't coursing as quickly through his system, what might he do when it is?

"I still felt pumped even though I knew it wasn't a save situation," he said. "I had a couple, three, days without throwing, so I just tried to come into this situation and go pitch."

At his own locker a few minutes earlier, Montero was asked about the fastest he's caught.

"Him, probably him," Montero replied. ■

With the acquisition of closer Aroldis Chapman, the Cubs demonstrated the club's total commitment to postseason success. (Joe Lewnard/Daily Herald)